Dedication

This textbook is dedicated to graduate students enrolled in my Human Learning Class, with a personal dedication to my deceased colleague Dr. Bernadette Francisco, who inspired me to complete this textbook.

Contents

List of Figures and Tables

Foreword

Many African-American males have developed or adopted alternative ways and styles of coping with problems. These ways are frequently in conflict with the standards imposed by the school, and are frequently viewed as negative or destructive. Social skills training should be considered as an ongoing intervention strategy, where the boys are taught effective ways of internalizing their behaviors and assessing how their behaviors may negatively impact upon others.

Activities and creative games can be designed to improve social skills as advocated in social learning theories, such as modeling, observations, imitation, sharing, taking turns, and cooperating. These activities and strategies should be developed and infused throughout the curriculum. Teaching appropriate social skills to young African-American males appear to be a promising technique for improving pro-social skills. Appropriate social skills are essential for developing personal relationships and accepting the roles of authority figures at schools as well as in the community.

Social skills and behaviors are learned; therefore, they can be changed and modified. Proper social skills require that an individual evaluate a situation, choose the appropriate social skill strategy, and perform the social skill. Unfortunately, many young African-American males have not been exposed to appropriate social skill models or do not possess enough prerequisite skills, such as maturity and self-control, to successfully perform appropriate social skills. These issues and more have been addressed in this text, including strategies for involving parents and the community.

Preface

This social skills curriculum has been developed as a guide to assist educators in instructing young African-American males in determining what behaviors are acceptable and what behaviors are not acceptable in our society. It is also designed to assist individuals working in community agencies with responsibilities for working with young African-American males. Parents and other family members will find these strategies useful for follow-up activities from the school.

Socialization skills which are assessed as necessary for young African-American males to function successfully in society are highlighted. Social skills outlined in the text stress strategies needed for: (1) respecting the rights and privacy of others, (2) learning how to handle anger, (3) learning how to act in public places, (4) showing good sportsmanship, (5) taking responsibility for one's own actions, (6) encouraging self-control, (7) selecting alternatives to using profanity, (8) learning when to apologize, (9) selecting alternatives to telling lies, (10) dealing with individuals who hit or threat, and (11) dealing effectively with drug problems.

This book is written with this point of view in mind, it presumes that a basic understanding of instructional methods and procedures have been attained. It does not address all of the dimensions of a functional curriculum; neither does it overview all of the possible instructional activities to employ in teaching social skills to young African-American males. Rather, the book simply provides a framework for innovative educators to extrapolate additional methods and procedures for teaching appropriate social and interpersonal skills to young African-American males so that they may be productive and contributing members of our society.

Many of the materials contained in this book are a direct result of in-service presentations, consultancies with public schools, empirical research projects dealing with improving social skills of young African-American males, and conducting drug seminars for the Union Institute and University. Additional research studies are included for the reader's assessment and review.

Acknowledgments

The methods and procedures outlined in this social skills curriculum have been developed over a period of years. They were developed to address the critical issue of providing early social skills training to young African-American males. The author was of the opinion that a functional systematic approach to teaching social skills was needed in order to equip these boys for functioning successfully in society.

Compiling this textbook was not an individual endeavor. It would have been impossible to complete this awesome task without the assistance of others. A deep sense of gratitude is extended to the following schools in the Baltimore City Public School System and to my colleagues at Coppin State College in Baltimore, Maryland:

_ The Sinclair Lane Elementary School and its staff.

_ The Robert Coleman Elementary School and its staff.

_ Robert Coleman, Division of Exceptional Children, Baltimore City Public Schools.

_ Mrs. Lavania Fitzpatrick and Mrs. Beatrice Riley for proofing the manuscript.

_ And a special thank you to Mrs. Emma "Sisie" Crosby for her dedication in typing this manuscript.

George R. Taylor, Ph.D.

Chapter 1

Introduction

The severity and complexity of urban education problems have become so widely publicized that they may be considered common knowledge. It is readily recognized that there are many deep-rooted problems facing the educational system today. Problems plaguing the urban schools include drugs, violence, outdated equipment, apathy, low expectations by educators and students, classism, racism, communities that do not seem to care. Schools and school districts are ill equipped to address and resolve all the problems and challenges faced with daily (Wright, 1992).

A concerted community effort is needed to reverse the present trend. Interagency cooperation from the various human services departments is needed, headed by the school. Basic physical, social, and emotional problems must be addressed, minimized, reduced, or eliminated before children can be successfully educated.

Many deprived Black male children reside in substandard environments where they are denied appropriate mental, physical, and social stimulation. The culture and life styles of these communities impede normal growth and development in several key areas of functioning (Matsueda & Heimer, 1987; Butler, O., 1989; Hatch & Gardner, 1988; Tomlinson, 1988). The impact of these negative culture and life experiences have resulted in some alarming statistics.

Throughout history, many African-American males have faced adverse conditions. Wright (1992) and Ascher (1991) reported that the African-American males in America continue to be that of an endangered species. It is apparent from statistical data that the African-American community is in a crisis. For example, Shade and Edwards (1987, p. 123) have documented that 86% of Black youth live in poverty..., 1 out of every 22 Black American males will be killed by violent crime..., 51% of violent crime in the U.S. is committed by Black youth..., 1 out of every 6 Black males will be arrested by the time he reaches the age of 19..., 40% of Black children are being raised in "fatherless" homes. The reasons why these statistics are so high among Black males are multiple and deep rooted.

In a 1990 Criminal Justice Report, it was revealed that almost one in four African-American males in the age group 20-29 was under some form of Criminal Justice supervision (Thomas, 1995). In 1995, statistics reported by the agency changed from 1990. Data revealed nearly one in three (32.2%) of African-American males in the age group 20-29 (827,440) is under Criminal Justice supervision on any given day (Mauer & Huling, 1995). The disproportionate representation of Black American males in the Criminal Justice System is well documented (Sampson & Lauritsen, 1997; Cahalan, 1986; Beck & Mamola, 1998). Consequently, much of Chapter 1 has been devoted to addressing this issue.

Too many young African-Americans become entangled in the criminal justice system due chiefly to environmental influences (Meyer, 1992). Statistics compiled by the U. S. Department of Justice reported that based on current rates of incarceration, an estimated 28% of Black males will enter state or federal prisons during their lifetime, in comparison to 16% of Hispanic males, and 4.4% for White males. Drug usage has also been responsible for increasing the number of young African-American males incarcerated. According to the Department of Justice (1993) an estimated 58% of federal inmates in 1991 and 21% of state inmates were serving a sentence for drug offenses (Bureau of Justice Statistics   Criminal   Offenders   Status, http://www.ojp.usdoj.gov/bjs/crimoff.htm). According to Mauer and Huling (1995) African-American males constitute 13% of all monthly drug users, they represent 35% of arrests for drug possession, 55% of convictions, and 74% of prison sentences.

Frequently, social skills, grades, education, motivation, and know-how area absent. These are skills needed to help them live a law-abiding life and to bring them some measure of success and personal fulfillment. Hilliard (1998) summed up the blight of urban education in this country by stating "nothing in school reform reports and effective research in general offers promise for the massive changes in education necessary to save the huge number of children in our systems who are at-risk. He concluded that the most at risk segment of the school population is the Black Male."

Fortunately, not all young Black males exhibit the aforementioned traits. A significant percentage of young African-American males are not at-risk. They live in environments that promote self-esteem and self-activity with appropriate models to emulate. The home environment provides the necessary support and love necessary for appropriate social and emotional development (Ayers, 1989; Kagan, 1989). Intervention and strategies outlined in this book are designed to improve interpersonal skills of at-risk young African-American males.

A Holistic Approach

Some young African-American males are being educated in substandard schools in most urban school districts. We have not done a satisfactory job of providing quality education for these individuals, the schools have failed to educate the "whole child." A recent report by the National Association of State Boards of Education (1992) noted that a holistic view that is attuned to the student's nonacademic needs must be included as part of his/her instructional program. This includes social, emotional, and personal citizenship training.

Instruction that minimizes the teaching of social and civic responsibility in the quest for academic excellence may not produce well-informed citizens in our society. Other researchers have voiced similar concerns (Bilken, 1990; Forest, 1990; Barth, 1990; Eisner, 1991; Lutfiyya, 1988; O'Brien & O'Brien, 1991) in support of a holistic integrated approach to educating children. It was recommended that to avoid fragmenting school experiences, students' social and emotional well-being must be integrated and infused into a total program emphasizing social and interpersonal needs, communication needs, and academic needs. The schools must begin to use the vast amount of research presented to experiment with various ways of including social skills development into the curriculum if young African-American males are to achieve their maximum potential.

The concept of teaching the whole child has been advocated since the beginning of this century. Historically, the school has mainly focused on academics, not the emotional development of children. However, a body of research draws attention to the importance of emotions in teaching children. Attention, learning, and memory are all associated with one's emotions. This concept does not appear to be readily understood by educators; thus, it is not adequately reflected in the curriculum. The school should conduct empirical studies showing the relationship between an emotionally positive classroom and the academic achievement and emotional health of pupils (Kandel & Kandel, 1994; Vincent, 1990).

The emotional system is a complex process under the direction and supervision of the brain. It is frequently viewed as a more powerful determinant of our behavior than our rational processes. Our emotional system is a complex, widely distributed, and error-prone system that defines our basic personality early in life, and is quite resistant to change. The clear implication of this research is that positive models and early interventions are needed if healthy emotions are to emerge. A detailed discussion of the emotional system is outside of the scope of this text.

The educational application of emotional research is still in its infancy. Since the concept is so important; however, some general principles to guide classroom applications are provided:

_   We should seek to develop forms of self-control among students and staff that encourage nonjudgemental, mental disruptive venting of emotions.

_   Schools should focus more on metacognitive activities that encourage students to talk about their emotions and listen to their classmates' feelings.

_   Activities that emphasize social interaction and engage the entire body tend to provide the best emotional support.

_   School activities that draw out emotions-simulations, role playing, and cooperative projects - provide important contextual memory prompts.

_   Emotionally stressed school environments are counter productive because they can reduce students' ability to learn.

Cummins (1984) findings also supported the notion of educating the whole child based on assessment of instruction models currently used by public schools to educate minority individuals. These models are most likely based upon cognitive theories and include (1) analysis of academic tasks, (2) establishment of sequential learning objectives based on each task analysis, and (3) direct instruction of individual task components. Most instruction and teaching in the public schools are based on the aforementioned models (Tharp, 1989; Poplin, 1988).

African-American males have different learning styles and frequently cannot achieve success with these traditional models; which often do not consider the learning styles or intergrated social skills experiences needed for young African-American males to experience school success. For example, some learners focus on global aspects of a problem while others focus on specific points. Ideally, a student should be flexible enough to do both. However, since schools traditionally give more weight to analytical than to holistic approaches, the student who does not manifest analytical habits is at a decided disadvantage (Hilliard, 1989). It is abundantly clear from the research that schools are not attuned or designed to educate young African-American males. Radical intervention models are needed, therefore, that stress social skills and interpersonal skills development. The schools cannot accomplish this awesome task alone, however, deep-seated societal problems must be addressed concurrently with education and educational problems, such as early environmental and home intervention strategies.

Early Environmental Experiences

Children born in poverty and neglect often suffer from deprivation that seriously impairs their abilities to learn. Early prevention programs for those at-risk children and their parents (starting with prenatal care and including health care, quality daycare, and preschool education) help prevent debilitating later educational efforts (Butler, 1989).

A key reason why some Black and deprived children have such a high rate of educational failure is that they often lag in physical and psychological development and may be unprepared to meet the demands of academic learning. For example, there is evidence to support that the lack of early experiences can affect brain development. Some areas of the brain require stimulation at the right time in order to take on their normal functions. Case studies of deprived and Black children indicate that there may be critical periods of cognitive and language development (Hatch & Gardner, 1988). Therefore, intervention in the early years appears to be the most effective way to improve the prospects for deprived children to receive maximum benefits from their educational experiences.

Impoverishment of a child's early environmental experiences, including any major restrictions on play activities or lack of feedback from older individuals, is suspected of retarding his/her social development and learning. Lack of adequate adult stimulation in the early years can lead to development of negative social behavior, which may be irreversible. First, the absence of adequate stimulation and activity, neurophysiological mechanisms involved in learning may fail to develop. Second, conditions in impoverished environments, such as the slums, generally do not provide sufficient variety and duration of exposure to perceptual-motor experiences compared to more affluent environments (Dalli, 1991; Dewitt, 1994).

Children learn violent behaviors early. We need to start with the 3 year-olds and teach them more appropriate ways to handle frustration, such as thinking about consequences of behaviors and decisions.

Home Environment

According to Butler (1989) children born into poverty and neglect often suffer from debilitating deprivations that seriously impair their ability to learn. Hamburg (1992) indicated that early prevention programs for these at-risk children and their parents reduce educational problems during the school years. Intervention in the earliest years is the most cost-effective way to improve the prospects of disadvantaged children. Early intervention programs should stress interpersonal relationships and drug education (Refer to chapters 5, 6, and 8).

Individuals are influenced by the elements within their environments. As a result, if we live in an environment that is a good match for our needs and abilities we will likely be more productive and prone to stay and will achieve academically. Individuals in mismatched environments, such as deprived Black children, often have trouble transferring values from one environment to another; therefore, many leave school when they reach the legal age. All children, including Black children, learn a great deal outside of the classroom. They have accomplished a vast amount of nonacademic learning before they enter school and continue to learn from nonacademic sources while they are enrolled. Historically, the schools have not tapped this great learning resource. Values, styles, and concepts that deprived Black children bring to the schools must be matched and integrated into their own social reality if school experiences are to be meaningful.

Research reported by Erikson as early as 1959 supported the notion that environments characterized by mistrust, doubt, limitations, and feelings of inferiority and powerlessness contribute to identity confusion and inhibit the development of the mature individual (Erikson, 1959). In support of Erikson's view, Ayers (1989) wrote that children need the home base of family life in order to grow up healthy and strong. They need to be listened to and understood, nurtured, and challenged by caring, committed adults. Parents need to contribute to their children's self-esteem, self-activity, or self-control through appropriate modeling strategies.

If a child's early development and early home environment are both low, there is an increased likelihood of poor developmental outcomes. The home environment is the foundation for further development within the child. Thus, it should be where the child receives support, experiences love, and acquires important skills towards becoming a productive, happy, social and emotional person. Experiences from the home need to be integrated with the school curriculum for meaningful experiences to occur, which will necessitate including the family and the community in the education process (Kagan, 1989).

Many young African-American males live in substandard environments where they are denied appropriate mental, physical, and social stimulations. These conditions impede normal development in all areas of functioning. Consequently, direct and immediate intervention must be made in the social environment of these children if they are to profit sufficiently from their school experiences.

Early Intervention Legislation

P.L. 99-457 (Part H Infants and Toddlers Program) is designed, in part, to offset some of the deprivation discussed here by assisting states in setting up early intervention programs for children from birth through age 21. Early intervention services include physical, mental, social and emotional, language and speech, and self-help skills. Special education services may be provided to children from birth through age 21 who have special needs, such as a physical disability, partial or total loss of sight, severe emotional problems, hearing or speech impairment, mental handicap, or learning disabilities. The key is early intervention, which should be designed to treat, prevent, and reduce environmental factors associated with disabling conditions and the impediment of social growth and development.

P.L. 99-457 was greatly needed due to the public dissatisfaction with earlier legislation created for the disabled. There was also a need for early care and education not just for the disabled child, but for the healthy child. Two factors contributed to the search for early childcare services: (1) the increase in the number of mothers who were working outside the home, and (2) the realization that many of these children were disadvantaged or from culturally different families and often not developmentally ready for school (Gallagher, 1989).

Kagan (1989) supported the issues addressed in P.L. 99-457, and further argued the importance of having early care and education of children go beyond the school doors. Again, emphasis was placed on including the family and the community in the educational process of children. Kagan's arguments for including the family and community stem from the realization that children are coming from more fragmented families, yet the technological advances of today's society require more complex environments. As a result, it is now more important than ever that the child is building on one stage of development to another by accomplishing certain learning tasks and by proceeding from the simple task to the more complex.

Transforming the Environment

A major factor affecting how well we function in our environment is self-esteem. Promoting self-esteem among children assists in reducing problems that otherwise may surface later in life. Several authorities have advocated the need for additional research in this area to evaluate the impact of strategies and programs designed to promote self-esteem (Butler, 1989).

Although we still need empirical data on the effectiveness of programs to raise self-esteem among children, high self-esteem appears to promote confidence, security, citizenship, and academic success. Recommended strategies or principles for improving self-esteem include.:

_ Praise rather than criticize.

_ Teach children to set achievable goals.

_ Teach children to praise themselves and to capitalize on their strong points.

_ Teach children to praise others.

_ Set realistic expectation levels.

_ Teach children to have confidence in themselves.

_ Praise children for achieving or failing after attempting to achieve.

_ Praise children for successfully completing a test or project.

_ Praise children for positive criticism.

_ Accept pupils' contributions without judgment.

_ Listen to children; they have important information to share.

_ Maintain a "you can do it" philosophy.

_ Present challenges for children.

_ Provide movement and freedom within the classroom for children to achieve objectives.

_ Demonstrate and show respect for children.

_ Listen to how you talk to children.

_ Catch someone doing something right and tell him/her about it.

_ Attack the behavior, not the student; separate the behavior from the child.

_ Use modeling or other techniques to reduce maladaptive behavior.

_ Teach children to respect themselves and others.

_ Teach children to be proud of their heritage.

_ Provide activities that incorporate involvement.

These strategies are not conclusive and should be expanded as assessed by the teachers.

Enhancing Self-Esteem of Young African-American Males

Due to the various factors within society and the community, the schools' role in enhancing self-esteem is of prime importance. Intervention must be made early to break or prevent failure due to low self-esteem. Thus, there appears to be a positive relationship between self-concept and student's success or failure in school (Taylor, 1993).

Many factors influence the young African-American male's development prior to going to school. When the school accepts the child, it should be committed to accepting and attempting to teach the whole child, not just developing the three R's. A major factor in children's development in the beginning school years is the view of themselves as they communicate with other students. For young African-American males, as well as other students, self-concept influences the motivation to learn. If students do not feel good about themselves generally, and good about themselves specifically as learners, they will lack the motivation to improve their performance in many academic areas. Group and individual activities are needed in order to improve the self-concepts of young African-American males. Specific activities have been developed to improve self-concepts in chapter 9.

The role of the teacher in promoting self-control cannot be overemphasized. Specifically, the teacher exerts considerable influence on a child's self-concept through the types of treatment, beliefs, and expectations that are upon the child. Children quickly react to and interpret negative traits projected by the teacher. The child's interpretation of the teacher's actions and their significance plays an important role in how the child reacts.

Children sift, seek, reject, and avoid information from individuals they do not respect or trust. Thus, they do not accept information from adults who have rejected them as readily as they do from adults who they feel have accepted them and seem trustworthy. Teachers can exert significant influence on the forming of the child's self-concept by constructing nurturing and positive learning environments, as well as showing positive attitudes and developing rapport with children.

Children's socioeconomic status should have no affect on how teachers judge their ability to learn. Teachers who classify children into social class memberships tend to show their prejudice toward selected groups of children. One major condition for enhancing self-esteem in the classroom is the teacher's acceptance of the chid. By accepting the child, the teacher indicates to the child that he/she is worthy of his/her attention and respect.

Another condition that promotes self-esteem is the presence of explicit limits in the classroom that are spelled out early and are consistently enforced. Such limits should involve input from the children. They should define acceptable behavior, provide standards of conduct, and establish behavior expectations in the classroom and school. Standards and regulations are necessary for children to develop positive self-esteem because they set limits and expectations.

A child's personality is organized around various aspects of self-awareness and self-concept. The structure of the school and the teacher's behavior greatly impact personality development. What we believe about ourselves affects what we do, what we see and hear, and out ability to cope in the environment. That is, self-concept is significantly influenced by life experiences due chiefly to the fact that it is learned, much of it through modeling. Young African-American males who have Black male teachers have better self-concepts than boys who have female teachers (Mancus, 1992; Ingrassia, 1993; Lapoint, 1992). Collectively, these studies suggest that the presence of Black teachers in the classroom provides a positive role model for the boys to emulate.

McRay's study (1994) supported the above premise. In a study involving young African-American males, he sampled both White and Black teachers' opinions of whether race made a difference in teaching young African-American boys. Seventy-two percent of the subjects responded that race make a difference in teaching young African-American males.

It is the view of this author that Black role models for young African-American males to emulate are very important; however, they should not be the sole criterion for predicting or determining success. Further, teachers who have a genuine interest in these boys, and who provide stimulating learning experiences, regardless of race or sex, can and will promote positive self-concepts. The key ingredient appears to be early intervention to compensate for negative early experiences. Many of the early life experiences of young African-American male children are negative and fail to provide opportunity for the self to emerge successfully. Consequently, many of these boy's self-concepts are lower than those of their healthy peers. By the time many young African-American males attend school, their attitudes toward school is well entrenched. Unfortunately, many of these attitudes are negative.

If these boys are to achieve successful academic progress, the school must develop interpersonal and social skills strategies that enable them to feel better about themselves. In some instances, social skills should supercede academic skills. Appropriate social skills must be taught and modeled for many of these children before a meaningful academic program can be pursued.

Not only are social skills important in academic areas; they are also related to socialization. Several behaviors are necessary in the socialization process, including the emergence of self-identity and self-concept. While social skills are developed through interactions with family, school, and the community, nothing is as important as the role of the parents. Parents provide the model for self-acceptance and the feeling that life is worthwhile. Also, parents who demonstrate a positive self-concept and high self-esteem treat their children with respect and acceptance and provide them with support and encouragement.

A child's social skills are shaped by the reinforcement he/she receives as a result of an action in the environment (Wood, 1984). Lack of social development diminishes the social status within the group (Anita & Kreimeyer, 1992; Odom & McEvoy, 1988; Peck & Cooke, 1983). Environmental conditions that nurture negative and aggressive behaviors must be transformed. To this end massive financial, social, and psychological support must be provided early. A coordinated community effort is needed to offset the present conditions in many urban communities in this country.

Summary

Individuals are products of their environments. They imitate experiences to which they have been exposed. Personality is conceived as a product of social learning. Its development is largely a function of the social conditions under which one grows up. There is frequently a conflict between these children's social values and the expectations of the school. This is chiefly due to the school not being tolerant of the cultural and behavioral styles of young African-American male children. Appropriate social skills should be taught and modeled for them before a meaningful academic program can be pursued. Since many of the habits developed by African-American males are well entrenched by the time they enter school, surface attention will not have a significant impact on changing negative habits. Instead, a coordinated and integrated program is needed. This book was designed to accomplish such a purpose. Actual classroom practices based upon field testing are stressed throughout the book.

Chapter 2

Social Learning Theories: An Overview

During the last two decades we have witnessed the rediscovery, creation, or validation of a diversity of social learning theories. These theories have provided us with a common language with which we can communicate about the affects of social learning theories of academic performance of minority and deprived children.

The study of social learning theories enables the schools to better understand both how young African-American male children think about school-related processes and how they likely feel about themselves in relation to the process. The school's understanding of both the cognitive and the affective characteristics of deprived children may be termed "empathic." One way of showing empathy to children is by designing effective classroom environments that consider the cognitive and affect levels of the children (Butler, 1988; Hilliard, 1989).

Theoretical Framework

The major emphasis of social learning theories is on environmental learner interaction. The learning behaviors that are socially accepted, as well as those that are not, is "social learning." This view is supported by Stuart (1989) who maintained that social learning theories attempt to describe the process by which we come to know what behaviors should or should not be projected when we are in different types of social situations.

The theories themselves are learning theories that have been applied to social situations. Generally, therefore, they have been behavioristic rather than cognitive (Bandura, 1977). These theories do not separate the parts from the whole; instead they have as a major underlying concept the holistic and interactive nature or development. For example, the various areas of the self do not exist or develop separately from one another, and movement toward maturity in one area can affect movement and learning in another area. Social learning theories also address individual differences and how such factors as personality temperament and sociological influences may interact with the developmental process.

Learning theories assist us in identifying how different individuals may manage, delay, progress through, or retreat from developmental tasks. These theories also suggest that there are persistent individual differences such as cognitive style, temperament, or ethnic background that interact with development. Additionally, these theories provide knowledge about individual types and styles that may be critical to our understanding of differing sources of reward and punishment for students (Stuart, 1989).

Vygotsky's Theory

Vygotsky's theory, according to Moll (1991) lends support to the concept that natural properties as well as social relations and constraints make possible the social construction of a child's higher psychological processes. The three major components of Vygotskian theory are: (1) the internalization of auxiliary culture means, (2) the interpersonal, or social process of mediation, and (3) a child's knowledge is formed within the zone of proximal development, a cognitive space defined by social relational boundaries.

One of the major tenets of Vygotsky's theory (Moll, 1991) is that there is a functional relationship between the effects of the culture on cognitive development and biological growth. Whereas the physical, biological, and neurological determinants are more readily understood and agreed upon, the impact of the cultural determinants is not easily understood. Cultural determinants include social processes which transform naturally through the mastery and use of culture signs. In essence, the natural development of children's behavior forms the biological conditions necessary to develop higher psychological processes. Culture, in turn, provides the conditions by which the higher psychological processes may be realized.

Commonality Among Theories

The common threads uniting these theories and concepts are imitation, modeling, and copying behaviors (Bandura & Walters, 1963). As do all children, young African-American males imitate, model, and copy behaviors directly from their environments. Recently, these models have become inappropriate and often create conflict and tension between children, society, and the school. Therefore, learning, culture, and behavioral styles of African-American males should be, as much as possible, incorporated and integrated into a total learning packet. Social learning theories provide a concrete framework for society and schools to begin implementing additional social skills strategies into the curriculum. "Social skills" is a term used to describe a wide range of behaviors varying in complexity and is thought to be necessary for effective functioning and academic success (Obiakor, 1990, 1991, 1992). Behaviors that constitute social skills development may vary depending upon the situation, role, sex, age, and disabling conditions.

Integrative Aspects of Social Skills Development

As indicated throughout this text, one major reason why young African-American males' behaviors are frequently rejected by schools and social institutions maybe attributed to their failure to display appropriate social skills needed for different social interactions. Various types of social skills instruction must be developed and systematically taught to young African-American males. The earlier the intervention, the sooner negative behaviors can be addressed. As indicated in Chapter 1, both the home and the school should play dominant roles in developing pro-social skills due to several factors associated with the urban environment.

The school may be the most appropriate agency, along with parental input, to conduct the social skills training or intervention. Teaching students pro-social skills necessary to cope with the social demands of society creates a climate in which positive relationships can exist and where students can be empowered to direct their own successes. A safe, supportive environment tends to facilitate learning. Pro-social skills taught and practiced daily in a nurturing environment assist in reducing negative behavior and in promoting positive ones (Taylor, 1992).

Social skills are developed through interactions with family, school, and community, and are shaped by reinforcement received as a result of such interactions. Often children do not learn effectively from past experiences. Frequently, they are enabled to transfer one socially accepted behavior to another social situation, thus, their behaviors are frequently interpreted as immature, inept, or intrusive. This negative feedback prohibits future social interactions. This is especially true for young African-American males.

Research findings suggest a significant relationship between social skills intervention and academic achievement. Thus, many social skill procedures, such as attending and positive interaction techniques, have been shown to increase academic performance. According to Oswald and Sinah-Nirbhay (1992) social skills interventions appear to work best when they correspond to actual interactions in the naturalistic environment. Similar findings by Walker, Irvin, Noell, and Singer (1992) indicated that some individuals do not have sufficient social skills to be successful in school. Finally, Walker (1992) stressed that there is an urgent need for social skills training that is integrated into the curriculum

Lack of appropriate social training may not permit many young African-American males to engage productively in social events. Findings by Kunjufu (1984) and Lloyd (1978) stated that young African-American males began to slide academically before the third or fourth grade. Special techniques and intervention related to remediating poor or inappropriate skills must be addressed early in their school experiences in order to bring their social skills up to acceptable school standards. According to Holland (1987) and Ayers (1989) early intervention is needed to expose young Black males to appropriate social models.

For many, their culture experiences have not provided appropriate social skills for them to be successful in the larger community or cope with appropriate social behavior. Changing inappropriate social behavior involves infusing principles of social learning theories such as modeling, imitation, and behavioral techniques with social skills instruction. Once social skills deficits have been identified, the social learning principles may be used to reinforce or reward appropriate social behavior.

Social Skills Models of Young African-American Males

Research findings have demonstrated that diverse groups of children, such as young Black males, are at-risk for developing inappropriate interpersonal skills (Taylor, 1991; Berry & Asamen, 1989; Clark, 1991). Thus, social skills deficiencies are commonly observed in this population. Several factors may attribute to these deficiencies such as child-rearing practices, deprived cultural environments, and lack of understanding of social expectations or rules. In turn, such deficiencies may lead to inappropriate or inadequate social behaviors.

Since social skills are learned throughout a lifetime from imitating or modeling both negative and positive behaviors, many individuals lack basic interpersonal skills if deprived of appropriate models. These individuals are frequently at a disadvantage in society and tend to feel inadequate and use unproductive and unacceptable ways of relating and communicating with others.

The importance of interpersonal skills instruction has been minimized in the schools. Mastering these skills requires training and practice. Interpersonal skills training allows children to recognize appropriate social behaviors, understand individuals' responses to certain behaviors, and respond appropriately. Lack of these skills often leads to feelings of rejection and isolation in a classroom or any public setting.

Beyond the areas discussed here, there is also ample evidence to suggest that children's social difficulties may emanate from different sources and areas. Such areas must be identified and remediated during the early years. Schools must design direct and immediate intervention programs that will permit young Black males to experience success (Butler, 1988; Hilliard, 1989; Kagan, 1989; Diggory, 1990; Foster, 1986; Deal, 1990; Holland, 1987; Ayers, 1989).

Teaching Anger and Hostility Control

Studies have consistently shown that negative behaviors such as anger and hostility are learned behaviors that children imitate from their environments. These behaviors manifest themselves in hostile and destructive patterns of behavior, which frequently cannot be controlled by the schools, thus, creating conflict and tension between children, parents, and the schools (Matsueda & Heimer, 1987; Gibbs, 1988).

Constructively expressing anger and hostility requires a great deal of inner control. Internal awareness of anger must first be established. If one is not aware of anger, it cannot be controlled. When anger is repressed or ignored, it will surface later and add to one's frustration. Further, usually by that time, anger is expressed in aggressive behaviors, such as attempts to harm someone, destroy something, make insults, and hostile statements. Aggressive behaviors manifest themselves in ways that infringe upon the rights of others.

Controlling anger and managing feelings are essential in developing appropriate interpersonal skills. Children should be taught how to control anger through application of the following:

1. Recognizing and describing anger.
2. Finding appropriate ways to express anger.
3. Analyzing and understanding factors responsible for anger.
4. Managing anger by looking at events differently or talking oneself out of anger.
5. Learning how to repress feelings.
6. Expressing anger constructively.
7. Experimenting with alternative ways of expressing.

A variety of strategies may be used to assist pupils in controlling or reducing anger. Role playing, creative dramatics, physical activities, timeout, relaxation therapy, writing and talking out feelings, assertive behavioral techniques, managing provocations and resolving interpersonal conflicts through cooperative approaches are but a few techniques that teachers may employ.

Teaching Apology Strategies

Apologies can restore relationships, heal humiliations, and generate forgiveness, if taught appropriately. It is a powerful social skill, but is generally not considered to be important by the school. It may be concluded, therefore, that the school views it to be a function of the home. However, as reflected throughout this book, the school must assume the leadership in teaching all social skills. This is especially true for a significant number of young African-American males, many of whom consider apologies to be signs of weaknesses, to display feminine traits, and admit failure. The few research studies reported indicate the reverse: Apologies require great strength, empathy, security, and strength (Taylor, 1992).

Failure to apologize can stain relationships, create grudges, and instill bitter vengeances. As mentioned, apologies are a show of strength because not only do they restore the self-concepts of those offended, they make us more sensitive to the feelings and needs of others. Like all social skills, appropriate ways to apologize must be taught.

Specific strategies have been outlined for teaching most social skills to young African-American males in chapter 9. Anger and hostility and the need to teach apology strategies have been observed and associated with many of the poor social skills shown by some young African-American males.

Harris (1992) concluded that many African-American males may have developed or adapted alternative ways and styles of coping with problems in their neighborhoods. These behavioral styles are frequently in conflict with the school and society in general, and may be viewed as negative or destructive. Behavioral styles and models copied and imitated by young African-American males may serve them well in their environments, but are frequently viewed as dysfunctional by the school and society.

The ability of low-achieving young African-American males to function satisfactorily in social groups and to maintain dispositions, habits, and attitudes customarily associated with character and personality is usually below levels set by the school. Thus, they are more likely than other children to be rejected by their peers, demonstrate fewer less rigid controls over their impulses, display learned hostile and destructive patterns of behavior, and often seem unable to respond to traditional classroom instruction.

Teaching Self-Regulation Skills

Instructional programs must be developed and designed to enable young African-American males to gain knowledge about appropriate interpersonal skills and to employ this newly acquired knowledge in solving their social problems. For this goal to be accomplished, these boys must be taught effective ways of internalizing their behaviors and assessing how their behaviors affect others. Helping young African-American males develop self-regulation skills appears to be an excellent technique for bringing behaviors to the conscious level where they can be controlled. Some of the more commonly used self-regulation skills are summarized in the following.

Be Aware of One's Thinking Patterns

Provide "think-aloud" activities and model how to solve problems by working through tasks and asking questions such as: (1) What is needed to solve the problem? (2) Things are not working out, should I try another way?, and (3) What assistance do I need to solve the problem?

As teachers perform these think-aloud activities, they may ask for input from the student relevant to the type of self-regulation skills being demonstrated. Skills may have to be modeled and demonstrated several times. Provide opportunities for the boys to demonstrate them individually and in cooperative groups, as well as to evaluate the effectiveness of their actions.

Making A Plan

Have the boys identify specific examples where self-regulation is useful. Motivation may come from a story, file, tape, or creative dramatic activities. Instruct the boys to develop a plan to reduce, correct, or eliminate the undesirable behaviors. As the boys demonstrate the behaviors, the teacher should reinforce and praise them.

Develop and Evaluate Long-Term Goals

Employ self-regulation strategies to assist the boys in accomplishing long-term goals. First have the boys identify social and behavioral goals. Record these goals and assist the boys in making a plan, as outlined previously. Schedule a time to meet with the boys to determine how well the goals are being achieved. In some instances, the goals will need to be modified or adapted such that they focus on specific behaviors. Self-regulation strategies make actions more controllable by making us aware of our own behavior. Once awareness is achieved, the plan outlined earlier may be taught to bring behaviors under control.

A variety of techniques and strategies may be used in developing self-regulation skills: (1) Role playing; (2) Classifying behaviors and identifying types of self-regulation strategies to employ; (3) Working in cooperative groups; (4) Positively reinforcing the mental habits; (5) Reading and developing stories; (6) Being sensitive to feedback and criticism; (7) Teaching self-monitoring skills; (8) Seeking outside advice when needed; and (9) evaluating progress.

Self-regulation is one of several strategies that may be used to teach appropriate social skills to young African-American males. Appropriate social skills are essential for developing personal relationships and accepting the roles of authority figures. Since social behaviors are learned, they can be changed and modified with appropriate intervention. They require that an individual evaluate the situation, choose the appropriate skills, and perform the social tasks appropriately (Katz, 1991). Unfortunately, many young African-American males have not been exposed to appropriate social models or do not possess enough prerequisite skills, such as maturity and self-control, to successfully perform the social skills. As mentioned, development of social skills in African-American males, as well as in all children, requires that they have appropriate models to copy and imitate, that they can recognize non-verbal clues, and that they adjust their behaviors accordingly.

The research of Matseuda and Heimer (1987) and Gibbs (1988) supports the findings of Katz (1991). These authors indicated that negative behaviors are learned behaviors which children imitate from their environments. The schools view these behaviors as hostile and destructive and respond in a negative fashion, thus, creating conflict and tension between schools and children.

Several researchers (Hilliard, 1989; Deal, 1990; Bilken, 1990; Taylor, 1992; Forest, 1990; Collins & Hatch, 1992; Kagan, 1989; Johnson & Johnson, 1990) have directly implied that social skills must be taught and integrated into the curriculum and assume a position of primacy along with the basic three R's.

Findings from other studies support these studies by concluding that many African-American males may have developed or adapted alternative ways and styles of coping with problems within their communities, which are frequently in conflict with the school and society in general and, therefore, are viewed as negative or destructive (Harris, 1992; Taylor, 1992; Hilliard, 1989).

Summary

Social learning theories offer the school a common context through which young African-American males' environment, developmental sequence, and early experiences can be understood and researched. Thus, these theories enable educators to better understand how young African-American males think and feel about themselves, thereby making them aware of factors in the environment that precipitate cognitive and affective problems that may have some bearing on academic performance.

The relationship between social learning theories and academic performance is not well established. Most research reported today simply indicates a causal relationship. There is a dire need to conduct empirical studies to determine what degree social learning theories impact on academic performance.

Social development is a major area in which many young African-American males need assistance, since they frequently have developed inappropriate interpersonal skills that are not accepted by the school. Inability to conform to expected social standards may result in unacceptable social skills, which are essential for developing personal relationships and accepting the role of authority figures (Taylor, 1992). Research findings by Hilliard (1989), Butler (1989), Holland (1987), and Johnson and Johnson (1990) support the notion that unacceptable social behaviors are directly associated with deprived cultural environments. Innovative ways must be found to provide appropriate role models for young African-American males to imitate and copy.

Chapter 3

Behavioral Styles of Young African-American Males

Introduction

As indicated earlier, many young African-American males have not mastered the social skills needed to be successful at school and within the larger community, resulting in frequent conflicts between the children and school on what is considered appropriate behavior. Much of this confusion can be attributed to the school's failure to understand the impact of various cultural styles on learning. Cultural values influence the behavior of individuals, including young African-American males (Bowman, 1994).

The powerful influence of cultural systems on cognitive style and behavior must be recognized and integrated into the instructional program of young African-American males (Hilliard, 1989). Curriculum planners must recognize that no one behavioral instructional strategy is appropriate for intervention. Rather, strategies should be selected based upon children's abilities and assessed needs as discussed in chapter 4.

Some of the learning preferences found to be characteristic of African-American learners include: (1) emphasize group cooperation; (2) value harmony with nature; (3) accept affective expression; (4) tend to be holistic or Gestalt thinkers; (5) perceive the field as responding to the person and as possibly having a life of its own; (6) use strong, colorful expressions; (7) require that relevant concepts have special or personal relevance; (8) use language that is dependent upon unique context and many interactional characteristics of the communicants–time and place, on inflection, muscular movements, and nonverbal cues; (9) prefer learning material that has a human social content and is characterized by fantasy and humor; and (10) perceived conceptual distances between the observer and the observed (Hilliard, 1989).

Consideration should be given to these characteristics when planning instructional programs for young African-American males. Each cultural style is different; however, similar characteristics operate across specific cultures. It is of prime importance that young African-American males be made aware of their cultural styles and how these impact and influence their learning. All curricula should reflect the richness and contribution of each culture.

The public schools should play a dominant role in multicultural education by including the contributions of diverse cultures. Historically, this has not ben the case. Instead, it was believed there was one dominant culture in this country, based upon the mores of Northern Europe. On this premise, minorities had to assimilate into the culture the best way they could. In the latter part of this century, culture views changed, however, advocates advanced and supported the notion that all cultures had significant contributions to make to our society. Strength in diversity was recognized. The school became the ideal social institution to advance the concept of diversity.

Through the introduction of multicultural education in the curriculum, young African-American males' self-perception will be enhanced and some of the stereotyping relevant to minorities and Blacks will be dispelled. As the self-images and concepts of young African-American males improve, they will have a source of identity and will gain excellent role models.

The Effects of Behavioral Styles

Styles is learned; learned patterns can be either changed or augmented, but cannot be ignored. Style tends to be rooted at a deep cultural level and is largely determined by prior experiences and motivation. Hilliard's research indicated that educational dialogue in recent years has given substantial attention to the importance and precise meaning of style in teaching and learning, particularly for minority groups. Thus, style differences between teachers and students and between students and the curriculum have been cited as explanations for the low academic performance of some minority groups (Hilliard, 1989).

Proper sensitivity to style can provide a perspective for enriching instruction of all children and for improving both teacher-student communication and the systematic assessment of students. The schools must become more sensitive to style out of basic respect for children and their tremendous potential for learning (Hilliard, 1989). Additionally, a person can use more than one style and can be taught to switch styles when appropriate. According to Deal (1990) the core problems of our schools today is not technical but spiritual and social. A climate for growth depends upon healthy, fertile social relationships where the styles and experiences of African-American children are recognized. The notion that each culture has made significant contributions to mankind should be highlighted and integrated into the curriculum (Bennet, 1988; Bank, 1991; Obiakor, 1992).

Correlating School Activities to Students Background and Ability

Upon entering school, children are regimented and required to follow specific rules that often conflict with their styles and modes of learning. Diggory (1990) further pointed out that the child and the school conceive of learning differently. The school is mostly concerned with verbal and written expressions and standardized test results. Many of these activities are foreign to children many of whom have not developed sufficient background or skills to master them. Behavior problems frequently occur due to differences between the child's ability and the expectations imposed by the school. If the school is to be successful in meeting the needs of children, especially those from diverse backgrounds, children must be given an active role in their own learning by structuring activities that are relevant and meaningful to them. Additionally, teachers must be free to experiment with various models of instruction (Taylor, 1992).

The role of the school should not be to fill children with information, but to help them construct understanding about what they are doing. Children's competence, their ability to make meaning from their environments, to construct knowledge to form generalizations, to solve problems, and to associate and transfer knowledge is seldom encouraged by the school.

The notion that style requires a specific pedagogical response, especially at the point of applying special teaching strategies, appears to be sound. It is widely believed that such an approach ought to be attempted and that teaching and learning will be more successful as a result. Students' cultural and learning styles appear to be inseparable; therefore, matching them with appropriate instruction appears to be a sound instructional strategy.

Learning Styles

Children receive and order information in different ways through a variety of dimensions and channels. Diggory (1990) implied that the school is not sensitive to the personal learning styles pupils have developed and mastered during the developmental stages. Making sense out of the world is a very real and active process. During early childhood, children master complex tasks according to their own schedules without formal training or intervention; the structured environment of the school appears to impede the personal learning styles of many children.

While there is no one common definition of learning styles, researchers have considered learning styles from four dimensions: cognitive, affective, physiological, and psychological.

Cognitive Dimension

The cognitive dimension of learning style refers to the different ways that children mentally perceive and order information and ideas. Witken (1975) analyzed cognitive style and determined how one's perception was related to information processing. A significant relationship was noted between abstract and concrete learners style of learning.

Affective Dimension

The affective dimension refers to how students' personality traits-both social and emotional-affect their learning. This dimension refers to how the student feels about himself/herself. What way can be found to build his/her self-esteem (Butler, 1988)? Learning styles are functions of both nature and nurture, and, according to Myers (1990) type development starts at a very early age. The hypothesis is that type is inborn, an innate predisposition like right-or left-handedness, but that the development of type can be greatly assisted or retarded by the environment.

Physiological Dimension

The physiological dimension of learning involves the interaction between the senses and the environment. Reynolds and Gerstein (1992) classified several channels under the physiological dimension, including (1) visual/auditory, (2) tactile/kinesthetic, and (3) a mixed combination of the five senses. The physiological dimension probes such questions as: Does the student learn better through auditory/visual or tactile/kinesthetic means? And how is the student affected by such factors as light, temperature, and room design? The physiological dimension involves the students' inner strengths and individuality.

Boys and girls process information through the physical channels differently. Specifically, prior to age 16, girls tended to have lower visual-spatial development and their brain developed earlier. Also, 10-12-year-old girls had twice the head growth of boys the same age, with boys catching up by the time they were 14 to 16. Also, girls were more sophisticated in language acts than boys the same age. Thus, sex and individual preferences play dominant roles in grasping and transferring knowledge.

Gregorc (1993) saw style as a way of viewing the world; a way of defining the mind's goals, content and cycles, and its differentiated mediation abilities of space and time. The mind's differentiated mediation abilities divide learning styles into sets that define one's reality base and ordering trends. According to Gregorc (1993) descriptors for the various learning styles include:

- Concrete Sequential - patient realist, instinctive, methodical.
- Abstract Sequential - serious, intellectual realist, logical, and analytical.
- Abstract Random - emotional idealist, perceptive.
- Concrete Randon - inquisitive, independent realist/idealist, impulsive.

Research findings strongly suggest that the dominant qualities of a learner's style are unchangeable. However, teachers can help learners be successful if they recognize their own style and use their strengths to teach toward their students' styles (Owens, 1991). Flexibility in working in the context of many styles within the classroom allows the teacher the opportunity to reach a variety of children with different learning styles. The benefits of such flexibility is immeasurable.

Finally, the issue of nature vs. nurture controversy has surfaced in the study of learning styles. Unlike Myers (1990) some researchers promote the impact of environment, others promote the impact of heredity, while many are neutral. There are advantages to using all approaches. The salient point is to keep the individual needs in mind as well as the modality favored.

Evaluating Learning Styles

Pupils learn through a variety of sensory channels and demonstrate individual patterns of sensory strengths and weaknesses. Teachers should capitalize on students' learning styles in their academic programs. Several aspects are recommended when considering factors that characterize a pupil's learning style:

5.   The speed at which a pupil's learning is an important aspect to consider. Learning rate is not as obvious as it may appear. Frequently, a learner's characteristics interfere with his/her natural learning rate. Although the learning rate is more observable than other characteristics, it does not necessarily relate to the quality of learner's performance. Therefore, it is of prime importance for the teacher to know as much as possible about all of a learner's characteristics.

6.   The techniques the pupils use to organize materials they plan to learn also need to be considered. Individuals organize materials they expect to learn information from by remembering the broad ideas. These broad ideas trigger the details in the pupil's memory. This method of proceeding from the general to the specific is referred as deductive style of organization. This principle may be applied successfully in many situations. Other pupils prefer to remember the smaller components, which then remind them of the broader concept, inductive style of organization. In utilizing inductive organization, the pupil may look at several items or objectives and form specific characteristics, develop general principles or concepts. Knowing a pupil's style of organization can assist the teacher in effectively guiding the learning process by presenting materials as close as possible to the student's preferred style or organization.

7.   The pupil's need for reinforcement and structure in the learning situation is also important. All learners need some structure and reinforcement to their learning. This process may be facilitated through a pupil's preferred channels of input and output.

8.   Input involves using the five sensory channels-auditory, visual, tactile, and kinesthetic, olfactory and gustatory- which are transmitted to the brain. In the brain, the sensory stimuli are organized into cognitive patterns referred to as the input channel through which the person readily processes stimuli as referred to as his/her preferred mode or modality.

9.   Similar differences are evident in output, which may be expressed verbally or nonverbally. Verbal output uses the fine-motor activity of the speech mechanism to express oral language. Nonverbal output uses both fine-and gross-motor activities. Fine-motor skills may include gesture and demonstration. Pupils usually prefer to express themselves through one of these channels.

10.   A pupil's preferred mode of input is not necessarily his/her strongest acuity channel. Sometimes a pupil transfers information received through one channel into another with which he/she is more comfortable. This process is called intermodal transfer. Pupils differ in their ability to perform the intermodal transfer. Failure to perform this task effectively may impede learning.

The differences in learning styles and patterns of some pupils almost ensure rewarding educational achievement for successful completion of tasks. Unfortunately, this is not true for many young African-American males. The differences reflected in learning can interfere with the pupil's achievement. Early identification, assessment, and management of a pupil's learning differences can prevent more serious learning problems from occurring.

Some children are concrete learners while others are abstract learners. Some focus on global aspects of a problem, others on specific points. Ideally, a student should be flexible enough to do both. Since schools traditionally give more weight to analytical than to holistic approaches, the student who does not manifest analytical habits is at a decided disadvantage (Hilliard, 1989).

Assessment of a pupil's preferred mode of input and output may be conducted through formal and informal techniques. A commonly used instrument is The Learning Channel Preference Checklist. This checklist along with two other instruments will be presented here.

The Learning Channel Preference Checklist

The Learning Channel Preference Checklist is designed for assessing learning styles. Teachers can administer the checklist and follow-up with interpretive discussions.

Students are asked to rank each statement as it relates to them. There are no right or wrong answers. Students rate each item as often (3), sometimes (2), and never (1), on three broad categories: visual, auditory, and haptic. The highest score indicates the preferred learning style in the aforementioned categories.

Auditory Learning Style. This is the least developed learning channel for all children, including most young African-American males

Visual Learning Style. Many children learn best when they can see information. High scores in this area denote that they prefer textbooks over lectures and rely on lists, graphs, charts, pictures, notes, and taking notes. A significantly higher number of children rate this area higher than the auditory channel.

Haptic Learning Style. This is the most frequently reported learning channel by children. That is, most children prefer this style. Haptic students show a cluster of right-brain characteristics. They learn best from experimenting rather than from textbooks.

The combined scores in the three areas usually range from 10 to 30. Often, two areas are close. Scores in the high 20s indicate that the student has satisfactorily developed all three channels and is able to use the modality that best fits the task. Scores below 20 indicate that the student has not yet developed a strong learning channel preference.

Usually, students scoring in the 20s have great difficulty with school because they do not have a clearly defined method for processing information. These students should be treated as haptic learners because the haptic style is much easier to develop than the others.

The checklist is a diagnostic tool, which indicates areas of strengths and weaknesses in sensory acuity. Based on this information, teachers can adapt or modify the instructional program to include activities that support the strongest modality. Information from the checklist should be shared with the student. O'Brien (1989) believed that all students can benefit from knowing their learning styles, as well as how to use and manipulate them in the learning process.

The Gregorc Delineator

Another instrument that deals specifically with learning style analysis is the Gregorc Style Delineator (GSD), which uses a four-channel approach to assess personality traits. The reliability and validity of the Gregorc Style Delineator in its present form can be characterized as strong. The manual carefully points out proper usage and cautions using the instrument in minority settings. When using the instrument in minority settings, it is recommended that one be sensitive to the cultural background of subjects. Thus, it is recommended that the reader carefully review the manual and consult expert opinion before using this instrument with minority individuals.

The Myers-Briggs Type Indicator

Another well-known instrument for assessing learning styles is the Myers-Briggs Type Indicator. The instrument assesses auditory, visual, and tactile acuity by asking individuals to repeat patterns using the above modalities. Results also show differences in cognitive strengths, such as holistic and global learning, in contrast to analytic, part-to-whole approaches.

These tests are culture and language specific. Individuals respond to an interpret self-reporting instruments based on their cultural experiences. These responses may be in conflict with established norms and, therefore, yield conflicting results. Consequently, caution is needed when interpreting results from minority individuals, especially young African-American males.

The Relationship Between Culture and Learning Style

Individuals from certain cultures show a preference for certain learning styles, and this preference may affect classroom performance. Schools must recognize, therefore, that students with diverse backgrounds have a favored learning style that may affect their academic performance.

When teachers fail to accommodate students' favored learning style in their instructional delivery, they may not meet students' individual needs. Hilliard (1989) supported the above analysis when he suggested that failure to match cultural and learning styles in teaching younger students is the explanation for the low performance of many culturally different minority-group students. He contended that children, regardless of their styles, are failing primarily because of systematic inequities in the delivery of whatever pedagogical approach the teachers claim to master-not because students cannot learn from teachers whose styles do not match their own.

Three cautions are recommended when attempting to match learning styles with cultural styles:

1.   Care should be taken when matching learning and cultural styles and not to make generalizations about a particular group based upon culture and learning styles. An example would be to conclude that all young African-American males have the same traits as the targeted group.

2.   Caution should also be taken in attempting to explain the achievement differences between minority and nonminority students; this is especially true when academic differences are used to explain deficits.

3.   One's philosophical beliefs and issues should not influence decisions relevant to the relationship between learning and culture styles.

Hilliard (1989) suggested in his research that the relationship between learning style and culture may prove to be divisive, especially as it relates to students in elementary and secondary schools. It may result in generalizations about culture and style and may lead to discriminating treatment. For example, it may be used as an excuse for student failure. Finally, there is an implication that some styles are more valuable than others even though learning style should be neutral. Properly used, however, matching learning and culture styles can be an effective tool for improving the learning of young African-American males.

The Relationship Between Learning and Instructional Styles

There is some indication that teachers choose instructional styles that closely approximate their own learning preferences. The key to the learning\instructional theory, however, is that students learn more effectively through their own preference in learning style (Hilliard, 1989).

Matching instructional and learning styles may also have implications for student achievement. The best way for schools to adapt to individual differences is to increase their effect by differentiated instructional techniques. According to Hilliard (1989) a careful match between learning styles and instructional styles may not be the only factor that affects student achievement. For example, the reason younger students do not learn may not be because they cannot learn from instructors using styles that do not match their learning styles, as well as instructors not being flexible enough to change their learning styles and teaching approaches. Additionally, there is not sufficient research or models to relate specific pedagogy to learning styles. Until appropriate instructional models are developed, he recommended that teachers be more sensitive to learning styles in the instructional programs.

Implications for Education

Traditionally, teachers teach and assess students in ways that benefit those with certain learning styles, while placing many other children at a marked disadvantage. Athanases (1993) noted that by keying teaching and assessment to the diverse ways people think and learn, teachers will be surprised at how much smarter their students get.

All individuals favor a preferred style; however, they may vary their styles depending upon the situation. Teachers should be flexible in their teaching and use a variety of styles to ensure that all students' needs are met. Teachers, generally, are best at instructing children whose styles of learning match their own. Consequently, the more students differ from the cultural, socioeconomic, or ethical values of the teachers, the greater the likelihood that their learning needs will not be met. Studies have shown that students receive higher grades and more favorable evaluations when their styles more closely match those of their teachers. Further, most students begin to experience success when they are permitted to pursue an interest in their preferred learning style (Athanases, 1993; Gregorc, 1993).

Summary

The preponderance of research on cultural and learning styles of minority individuals has demonstrated the value of matching these two styles to facilitate the learning process. It is widely believed that such matching can facilitate classroom instruction and provide young African-American males with the skills necessary to succeed in school. Despite some caution in matching cultural, learning, and teaching styles when applied to educating minority individuals, there is little disagreement in the professional literature concerning the relationship between learning and culture styles and their impact on academic and social success in school.

Research conducted over the last decade has revealed certain learning patterns as being characteristic of certain minority groups (Hilliard, 1989; Shade, 1989; Vasquez, 1991; Bert & Bert, 1992).

African-American groups, for example, tend to use oral experiences, physical activity, and interpersonal relationships over other approaches and patterns. The implications for instructional intervention for these individuals should be self-evident.

As indicated earlier, there is not universal agreement on the application of cultural and learning styles to instruction. Some advocate that applying cultural and learning styles to the instructional process will enable educators to be more sensitive to cultural differences. Others maintain that pinpointing cultural values will lead to stereotyping.

Another controversy evolves around the extent to which culture and learning affect achievement. Research findings have consistently pointed to serious inequities when schools do not value or accept certain cultural values. Some studies have shown that incorporating cultural and learning styles in the learning process does not significantly increase achievement unless inequities in delivery/instructional procedures are improved (Hilliard, 1989; Bennet, 1986).

A third controversy centers around how teachers operating from their own cultures and learning styles can successfully teach minority populations. Most of the research shows that caring teachers who provide opportunities for children to learn are more valuable than careful matching of teaching and learning styles (Taylor, 1992).

The major issues at hand in this controversy is now whether learning and cultural styles should be incorporated in the instructional plan for young African-American males, but whether information about cultural and learning styles will assist teachers in recognizing diversity and thereby improving delivery of educational services.

Chapter 4

Practical Application of Social Learning Theories to Educating Young African-American Males

Social learning theories offer the school a common context in which the environment, developmental sequence, and early experiences of young African-American males can be understood and researched. These theories enable the educators to better understand how these children think and how they feel about themselves. They also make educators more aware of factors in the environment that precipitate cognitive and affective problems that may have some bearing on academic performance.

The importance of teaching social skills to African-American males has been well documented. Thus, the preponderance of research strongly supports the notion of teaching and integrating social skills into the curriculum while emphasizing that social skills should assume a position of primacy along with basic three R's (Hilliard, 1989; Deal, 1990; Bilken, 1990; Forest, 1990; Collins & Hatch, 1992; Kagan, 1989; Johnson & Johnson, 1990).

Types of Social Skill Deficits

There are four major types of social skills deficits: (1) skill deficits, (2) inadequate skill performance, (3) performance deficits, and (4) self-control deficits.

1.   Skill deficits occur when individuals do not know how to perform the social skill in question.

2.   Inadequate skill performance implies that the individual has partly performed the social skill but, due to lack of understanding, has not completed it. An example may be when

somebody is blamed for an act he/she did not commit. Initially, the person would say he/she did not commit the act. However, when the other individual keeps insisting, the accused individual may resort to aggressive behavior rather than using negotiation strategies.

3.   Performance deficits indicate that the individual knows how to perform a given task but due to physical or other problems, does not complete it.

4.   Self-control deficits include a variety of behaviors in which the individual cannot control his/her behavior. A multitude of problems may be with this deficit. Frequently individuals have to be taught how to control their behaviors. (Specific techniques will be summarized in chapter 5.)

Effects of Social Skills Deficits

Social skills training should assume an important place in curricula for young African-American males. An increasing number of young African-American males fail to succeed in school because of inadequate social skills. It has been suggested that social skills deficits not only interfere with success in the peer group and educational mainstream, but are also predictive of long-term maladaptive behavior patterns including delinquency, dropping out of school, drug abuse, military discharge for bad conduct, and adult mental health problems.

As a result, acquisition of social communication skills is extremely important for these boys, primarily because social communication skills are the foundation of interpersonal competence. Inclusion of social skills training in curriculum and specific lesson plan design provides the classroom teacher with the opportunity to effectively address social skills deficits.

Research has shown that social skills training packages promote acquisition of socially appropriate behaviors, but there is little evidence to suggest that instruction directed at improving students' social competence transfers over time and across cultural settings. Several reasons for this generalization have been presented.

First, social interaction is reciprocal; it involves social exchange among individuals. The limitations and the absence of socially competent peers as models for young African-American males may seriously impair this reciprocity. Training must take place in settings where these students interact with their peers in order for newly acquired skills to be generalized and maintained.

Second, exposure to adequate peer model is insufficient; peers must be trained to provide appropriate models for young Black males (Holland, 1987). Further, social skills training and reinforcement must occur in settings in which these boys interact naturally with their peers (Taylor, 1994).

Third, young African-American males must be taught to exhibit behaviors that will be reinforced naturally by peers. Therefore, it is important to select target behaviors that are adaptive and desirable, contribute to the development of social competence, and prompt peer responses that are likely to be reinforcing. The lack of social skills training, inappropriate behavioral activity, and poor interpersonal relationship problems all result in deficits in social skills.

Research has shown a positive relationship between certain social skills and school achievement of young African-American males. For example, acts of social communication such as initiating contact about work assignments, asking and answering questions, and engaging in academic-related discussions are experiences needed for appropriate social exchange (Holland, 1987; Hilliard, 1989; Taylor, 1992). Teachers tend to place less value on these social communication skills, however; thus, few opportunities for development of social communication are likely to be provided in classrooms for young African-American males. Systematic assessment procedures are needed to aid the teacher in employing appropriate intervention strategies.

Assessing Social Skills

Several tests are available for assessing social skills of young African-American males. These tests measure all aspects of social behavior and may be classified as formal or informal. Since many of these tests were designed for different populations, they will have to be modified for use with young African-American males.

Assessing Social Skills Deficits

Several types of instruments may be used to assess social skills. Commonly used teacher-made tests use several testing formats. These include checklists, observation schedules, rating scales, interviews, direct observations, role play, assessment of social competence, and a variety of inventories covering the gamut of social behaviors. (Examples of assessment inventories appear in Appendixes B and C.)

Anecdotal records may also be used in obtaining data about pupils. These records provide an opportunity to study a pupil's behavior over a period of time as well as collecting information that is essential in planning instructional programs. Additionally, anecdotal records provide a means of understanding the dynamics of the learner over a period of time.

Taylor (1997) stressed the importance of assessing children's social skills during the early years using both formal and informal techniques. One of the techniques discussed is the Social Attributes Checklist. Areas covered in checklist include 8 individual, 14 social skills, and 2 peer relationship attributes. Results from the checklist pinpoint areas of social development in the above attributes that need to be addressed.

The Pediatric Evaluation of Disabilities Inventory is a measure of functional skills in the social function domain. It is also a checklist-type inventory. Haltiwanger (1992) used this checklist with a large sample of parents of young children. A major component of the study was to interview these parents to determine the amount of assistance they provided their children for each skill on the checklist. Analysis of the responses showed that children who were successful received at least minimal assistance or supervision from their parents.

Few tests are designed specifically to assess social skills of young African-American males. As indicated, most tests have to be modified to assess the social traits of this unique group of males. The reader is referred to the latest issue of Buros' Mental Measurements Year Book for additional tests.

Social skills are difficult to assess due chiefly to issues related to reliability, and interpretability. Many social skills are directly associated with one's culture and when assessed outside of that culture, results can be misleading. Assessment instruments for measuring social skills should be interpreted with the uniqueness of the individual in mind and the type of intervention that is being attempted to change the negative behavior.

Application of Behavioral Intervention Strategies

Learning depends upon the following factors: drive, response, cue, and reward. The principal theoretical concepts drawn from this assumption are reinforcement values and expectations. The tendency for behavior to occur in any given situation is a function of the individual's expectations of individual's expectations of reinforcement in that situation and of the value of the reinforcements.

The reinforcement values and expectations of some young African-American males differ from the values expected at school. Thus, what has been successful for them in their environments may be a source of conflict in the school. In essence, these children have frequently been reinforced by what the school may term "negative behaviors." The goal-driven behaviors, responses to events, and the cues they have developed are frequently a means of survival in their environments. These behaviors work well for them until they attend school. At school, the copying and imitative tendencies learned at home are generally not tolerated or accepted, causing frustration, poor self-image, and sometimes aggressive behavior (Villegas, 1991; Bronfenbrenner, 1979).

Most children can learn from rewards and punishments, and then proceed to make a judgement in a new social situation as a result of previous experiences (Greshan & Elliott, 1989). "Social referencing" involves using information from other people to guide behavior and affect ambiguous situations (Obiakor, 1992).

Unfortunately, many at-risk young African-American males cannot learn effective social skills without direct intervention. Frequently, behavior problems arise in class because successful intervention techniques have not been tried. Most traditional methods do not work for many young African-American males. A learning environment is needed that fosters reduction of negative behaviors and recognizes the uniqueness of the individual.

One intervention strategy that appeared to reduce aggressive behavior among males was used by Hudley (1993). A sample (101) of aggressive and nonaggressive elementary-school boys were randomly assigned to an attributional intervention and a nontreatment control group. The study was designed to determine the effects of an attribution intervention program on reducing aggressive male's tendency toward ambiguous negative peer interactions. Findings revealed that the experimental group of boys (attributional intervention) showed a significant reduction in hostile intent and disciplinary action as rated by their teachers (Hudley, 1992, 1993).

Research by Jewett (1992) focused on aggression and cooperation and ways of helping young children use appropriate strategies for coping with them. Jewett asserted that aggression and cooperation share one common element, which emerges from children's strong development push to initiate control, and maintain relationships with their peers.

Aggression was defined as any intentional act that resulted in physical or mental injury. Aggressive actions can be accidental, instrumental, or hostile acts of behavior. It was noted that aggression should not be confused with assertion. Assertion, in turn, was defined as a process or behavior through which children maintain and defend their rights.

Cooperation, on the other hand, was defined as any activity that involves willing interdependence of two or more students. Cooperation was distinguished from compliance in that compliance denoted obedience to authority rather than intentional cooperation. Aggressive behavior may be reduced by employing strategies that permit students to verbalize their feelings, develop appropriate problem-solving techniques to conflict, and internalize and be cognizant of the effects of their aggressive behaviors upon others.

Collins and Hatch (1992) summed up effective strategies for supporting social and emotional growth of young children: (1) model social behavior; (2) establish environments that encourage positive social exchange; (3) encourage children to become aware of the consequences of their behaviors; (4) help children produce acceptable behavior; and (5) encourage the development of children's self-esteem. These behavioral techniques are also designed to make individuals aware of their impact on reacting to and interacting with others.

Summary

One of the valuable roles of teachers is that of being an observer. Observing behavior in the classroom provides valuable information for intervention. Frequently, on the basis of the information supplied, appropriate action can be taken to change negative behaviors. The same rationale may be advanced for other interventions. Equally important is the interpretation of the information from assessment for young African-American males. It is recommended here that resource individuals knowledgeable about Black cultures be consulted before intervention is attempted.

Chapter 5

Drug Intervention Techniques Using Social Skills Interventions

Introduction

It is not within the scope of this chapter to trace the history of drug intervention, nor to report on all social intervention techniques used. The major thrust is to review techniques employed in the schools to combat drug abuse. The reader is referred to Hoffman, Harrison, and Belile (1986)[1], Miller & Chappel (1991)[2] for historical information.

National statistics indicate that addiction to hard drugs is on the increase for young African-American males. Nearly one in three (32.2%) of them in the age group 20-29 (827,440), is under Criminal Justice supervision on any given day, in prison or jail, or on probation or parole. Young African-American males constitute 13% of all monthly drug users. They represent 35% of all arrests for drug possession, 55% of convictions, and 74% of prison sentence (Mauer & Huling, 1995; Greenwood, 1992; Johnson, O'Malley, & Bachman, 1998; U. S. Government General Accounting Office, 1993).

The exact number of young African-American males using drugs is not known, since many of them are not apprehended or convicted. The increase in drug usage and abuse can be attributed to many factors; many are deeply rooted in the culture and various types of personality conflicts that many young African-American males experience in our society (Grob, DeRio, 1992; Newcomb & Bentler, 1988; Shedler & Block, 1990; Taylor, 1972). Whatever the reasons for the increase in using hard drugs, society faces a mammoth task in reversing this present trend.

Law enforcement is but one approach to minimize the growing drug abuse problem among this population. Preventing initial usage and rehabilitating users are other approaches which may be used (Martin, Duncan, & Zunich, 1983; Skager & Austin, 1998; Botvin, 1995; Goodstadt, 1989; White and Pitts, 1998).

Results from surveys conducted by Ponton (1997) and Brown (1997) show that motivation for drugs vary depending upon numerous factors. Among theses are: curiosity, peer influence, desire for kicks, escape from feeling of inferiority, frustration, psychological escape, emotional instability, rebellion against parental authority, and dissatisfaction with the educational process.

The results of a USA Today study revealed that African-American males are four times as likely as Whites to be arrested for drugs (Vincent, 1993). Percentage of drug offenders admitted to prison by race and by states is reported from the National Correction Reporting Program (1996).

Data in Figure 5.1 show the number of Blacks and White offenders admitted to prison by race. Data show that 18 states admitted to prison more Blacks than any other race for drug related crimes. Maryland and Illinois lead the Nation with 90% admission rate. Other states with high percentages included: South Carolina, North Carolina, Louisiana, Virginia, and New Jersey (Refer to fig. 5.1 for additional details).

The racial disparity in drug arrests is the result of the long focus on arrest and imprisonment instead of prevention and treatment for young African-American males. This disparity has created a self-fulfilling cycle of police suspicion and arrest throughout the country, festering racial tensions and resentment. Hutchinson (1999) articulated that the standard reasons given for criminalizing practically an entire generation of young Blacks is that they are poor, crime prone, and lack family values. He concluded that these trends may be summed up as racially biased drug laws.

Part of the solution to reduce these dreadful statistics is to provide job training and opportunities for these idle young African-

Figure 5.1 Percentage of Drug Offenders Admitted to Prison by Race

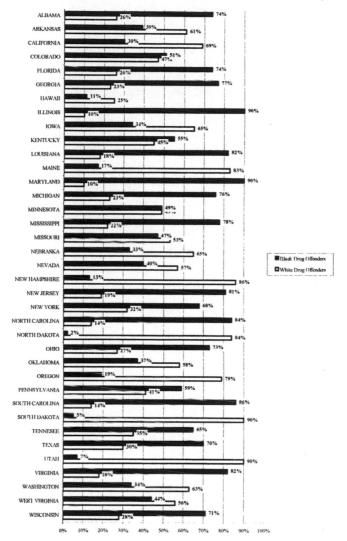

Source: Calculated from National Corrections Reporting Program, 1996 data.

American males, especially in the inner city, more anti-drug programs and diversion programs that get small time users treatment, not jail. A significant number of research studies have found a high correlation between the socioeconomic status of young African-American males and drug crimes.

Socioeconomic Factors and Drug Crimes

In an attempt to find some of the causes of the high number of young African-American males incarcerated, a number of studies found correlations between socioeconomic status, ethnicity/race, and drug/drug-related crime. Gordon, Gordon and Nembhard (1995) concluded an extensive review of the literature from 1955 through 1994 on African-American males and their involvement in a variety of social problems. It was concluded that studies focusing on demographic factors have repeatedly shown that urban, young, unemployed African-American males of lower socioeconomic status tend to cope with social conditions by drinking alcohol and/or using drugs. Also, many of these men also become involved in crimes that are drug-related.

In another study conducted in Cleveland, Pandey and Coulton (1994) found that as neighborhoods declined, when they become more populated by lower socioeconomic groups of minorities, soon drug-related crimes began to in crease as did the number of non-drug related crimes. It was also found that the incidence of drug/drug-related crimes was highest among young groups of the African-American sub culture away from the mainstream, dominant culture of white America.

Bailey, Hser, Hsieh, and Anglin (1994) studied minorities involved in drug crime by following 354 narcotics addicts remanded to the California Civil Addict Program from 1962 through 1964 for a period of 24 years. Self report data collected at initial treatment admission, and in two follow-up interviews (1974-75 and 1985-86), included information on family history, patterns of drug use, criminal involvement, socioeconomic status, and other behavioral and sociodemographic factors. Findings revealed that there were different kinds of addicts defined by the authors as: winners, striving addicts, enduring addicts, and incarcerated addicts. All but one of these categories was heterogeneous with respect to socioeconomic class. This category was that of the enduring addicts who commonly accessed methadone treatment and avoided incarceration while persisting in narcotic addiction and crime; findings of the study showed that almost all of the subjects in this group were of lower socioeconomic status.

Investigating factors related to robbery-associated assaults on police officers, Meyer (1992) found that assailants tended to be male, non-white, and to possess prior criminal records. Moreover, assailants came disproportionately from lower socioeconomic groups, with over 75 percent being unemployed. However, contrary to findings in general police assaults, only a small percentage of those involved in robbery-related assaults showed signs of mental derangement or were under the influence of drugs or alcohol. Thus, there are certain drug crimes that lower socioeconomic, non-white groups are more likely to be involved in than others.

Short (1997) concluded that there is a relationship between violent crime, drug crime, lower socioeconomic status, and young Black males and offers an explanation of this relationship. First, Short reports that the distribution of violent crimes associated with drugs is heavily skewed toward younger, poorer, male minorities. Community variables, such as the availability of job opportunities and the dominant beliefs and values transmitted in a neighborhood, are said to strongly interact with microsocial variables to produce this violent behavior.

Short (1997) further claimed that prominent among the effects of these community variables is the presence of unsupervised youth groups, or gangs. Short argues that gangs emerge in situations in which traditional kinds of social capital have eroded because of demographic and economic shifts that concentrate poverty and destabilize conventional community institutions. In such situations, Short states that:

> the legitimacy of adults associated with these institutions is weakened, and young people become more likely to resist adult authority. This situation breeds the conditions for violent behavior at the microlevel. Included in salient microlevel variables are the presence of early childhood disorders, alcoholism and drugs, marital discord, and impulsive and aggressive behavior. (p. 1)

A related explanation for the involvement of lower class African-American males in drug crime has been offered by Manwar (1997) who articulated that cross-cultural studies have found that children deprived of parental affection tend to become aggressive, and during the formative phase, these circumstances shape modal personality. He then goes on to note that in the inner cities of the U. S., especially in the African-American community, the process of identity formation is different from that in the mainstream culture, making the point that since poverty, social discrimination, violence, crime and drug use are prevalent in the inner cities, they play a vital role in the process of identify formation.

In particular, two kinds of structural conditions - economic and ideological - are said to determine youths' involvement with violence, crime, and drug selling/use. In this cultural environment, aggressive behavior, (e.g., counter hegemonic confrontation with the elite culture and equivocation of state control), are said to be viewed as powerful attributes for a person. And, Manwar (1997) stated it is this kind of identity that leads to the involvement of young, poor African-American males in drug crime.

Another explanation for the finding that young African-American males of lower socioeconomic status are involved in drub/drug-related crimes has been offered by Palermo and Simpson (1994) who reflect on the origin of the family and its traditional dynamic force in the social and moral education and in the effective support and protection of its members. In this regard, the authors note that since the institution of the family is progressively crumbling under the pressure of ever-changing socioeconomic events, people feel more insecure and frustrated.

As a result, the present day family is said to not pass on to its members those traditional high moral values of honesty and responsibility so important for good citizenship and self-esteem. It is further noted that when these values are not transmitted and when there is unemployment and the widespread presence of psychoactive drugs in the streets, this is a basic factor in the upsurge of violence and criminal behavior.

Even though violence in the streets is multifactorial and the too easy availability of guns and the drug culture are certainly important factors, Palemo and Simpson (1994) believe that the progressive disintegration of the family and its value deficit are basic to the problem of disruptive violence in the streets and also to the problem of drug crimes being frequently committed by poor, urban young African-American males.

Palermo and Simpson's (1994) argument finds some support in a study of drugs and crime in a sample of upper middle class adolescents (both African-American and White) conducted by Levine and Kozak (1979). Findings of the study indicated that the drug/drug related crimes committed by these young people ruled out the explanations usually offered to explain lower socioeconomic involvement in drug crime, e.g., unemployment, negative social conditions, and so forth.

Instead, it was found that considerable numbers of students report that their parents had not established certain regulations for them. Thus, the view advanced by the authors centered around deficient socialization and inadequate parenting as causes of these behavioral problems. However, since the study did not categorize the data in a way to permit cross-tabulations either supporting or invalidating this argument, this conclusion is a tentative one.

Earlier in this chapter, it was noted that most studies of drug crimes committed by African-Americans have restricted themselves to certain subset of the African-American population and/or to certain geographic areas (e.g., urban areas). However, some have made the argument that the indices chosen to determine involvement in drug crime (e.g., arrest and/or conviction rates) is an unfair measure. This is because these indices, at least in part, reflect the propensity of a racist society to arrest and/or convict African-Americans more frequently than whites - especially lower income African-Americans. Those advancing this argument would point out that while African-American males comprise only six percent of the American population, they constitute 50 percent of the prison population (Chiricos, 1994).

However, not all research supports this argument. For example, Klein, Petersilla, and Turner (1990) examined racial bias in court decisions controlling for the nature of crimes committed, prior record, other offender characteristics, and race. Data were analyzed for 1980 California offenders convicted of assault, robbery, burglary, theft, forgery, or drug crimes.

Findings for five of the crimes studied indicated that courts were making racially equitable sentencing decisions. Drug crimes were the exceptions; however, it was not African-Americans but Latinos who faced a higher probability of imprisonment. There was no evidence of racial discrimination in the length of prison term imposed for any of the crimes.

There is, however, some support for the notion of gender bias, at least as it relates to the handling of young people strongly involved in drug/drug related crime. In this regard, Horowitz and Pottieger (1991) investigated for gender bias in the handling of seriously delinquent youths at three stages of the juvenile justice system: arrest, adjudication, and disposition.

Subjects in the study were 391 African-American and White 14-17 year old youths (100 girls and 291 boys), all heavily involved in crime. These young people were interviewed on the street during the period 1985-1987. Results revealed a number of differences in male and female outcomes at all stages of the juvenile justice system. Thus, if there is bias, it is probably not being based on racist standards and criteria so much as sexist standards and criteria. Regardless of the reasons for the large number of young African-American males arrested on drug charges, bias appears to be the underlying cause whether it's socioeconomic, racist, or sexist standards. Poor socioeconomic factors can not be divorced from psychological factors. They work as an integrated whole in promoting drug usage.

Psychological Factors Associated with Drug Abuse

There are several psychological factors associated with drug abuse habits. These factors impact significantly upon treatments which impacts upon social development. Drugs have been found to have a severe impact upon psychological development of young African-American males, as well as other individuals. Psychological factors affect a wide range of relationships including: (1) parent-child interactions, where drugs influence positive communication between child and parent, (2) peer relationships influence drug related behaviors and place young African-American males at risk for experimenting with drugs, (3) adult role models like peer relations influence how children react to drugs. They frequently model the behaviors of adults they admire. Special social intervention strategies may be used to reduce, minimize, or eradicate the use of drugs which is rampant among young African-American males.

One key to breaking the vicious drug cycle is the education of young African-American males directed towards prevention of drug use and rehabilitation of drug users with emphasis on the causes and consequences of drug misuse and abuse. Social intervention should reflect the assessed social needs of young African-American males. For this purpose, teacher-made checklists may be used as outlined in Chapter 4. Several approaches may be used to reduce the use of drugs among young African-American males through the use of social intervention techniques.

McGinnis and Goldstein (1984) supported the concept of direct instruction of social skills, recommending modeling, role playing, practice, and feedback as principal procedures and techniques to teach social skills. Additional instruction using the techniques discussed in this chapter can facilitate the teaching of social skills through direct instruction.

"Direct instruction" implies that the teacher is directly intervening to bring about a desired change. Direct instruction is to be used with any subject area, including drug prevention and the harmful affects of drugs, to assist children in learning basic skills, as well as employing the concept of task analysis (step-by-step sequence of learning task).

Direct Instruction Framework

Bandura (1977) provided us with the conceptual framework for using direct instruction, advancing the concepts of Social Learning Theory and Behavioral Modeling. He advocated that much of what we learned is through modeling from observing others. Information that is carefully and systematically gained through modeling may be transferred to other academic, social, and nonacademic functions, such as drug education.

Specific techniques for using effective modeling and direct social skills training and interventions to reduce drug usage, will be delineated later in the chapter.

Reducing Drug Addiction Through Social Skills Intervention

The major theoretical notion underlying this approach is premised upon the belief that alcoholics have deficits in social graces and that it delimits the drug abuser's ability to deal appropriately with social issues with family, work, and interpersonal relationships with others. It is assumed through the use of these social intervention models, the desire for alcohol is reduced or controlled. Research finding by Chancy, O'Leary, and Marlatt (1978) have not validated the effectiveness of social intervention in reducing drug abuse. A great deal of the lack of validation of social skills intervention may be attributed to alcoholics participating in other programs which may have had a social intervention component, such as the programs outlined below.

Relapse Prevention

Marlatt (1973) is one of the major supporters of relapse prevention as a technique to be employed in treating alcoholism. A behavioral approach is used to reduce the causes which are viewed as precipitants in the relapse to alcohol and drugs. Other researchers support Marlatt's view in that they agree that reduced consumptions are seen as the measure for positive behavioral changes (Miller & Hedrick, Taylor, 1983).

Brief Intervention

This strategy is premised upon the patient and the therapist reaching an understanding relevant to an agreed goal concerning the patient's drinking habit based upon an agreed standard. The process is designed to assist the patient in reducing his/her drinking. Patients are expected to be realistic in selecting goals. Records are kept by the therapist and frequently reviewed with the patient.

Stress Management

Stress management is frequently combined with other forms of treatment such as aversion therapy (Blake, 1967; Sission, 1980). Aversion therapy, according to Boland, Mellor, and Revusky (1978); Jackson and Smith (1978); Glover and McCue (1972), is designed to produce an aversive reaction to alcohol by establishing a conditional response in an individual. The ingestion of alcohol is paired with a negative stimulus in order to produce automatic negative responses, such as nausea, apnea, electric shock, and imagery, when the patient is exposed to alcohol.

The above social intervention techniques are frequently administered by trained therapists. Many states require that the therapists are licensed to treat patients using some of the above strategies. Generally teachers are not trained to use those techniques in drug education programs. Social intervention techniques such as behavioral and cognitive approaches are most often used by teachers and educators in the classroom. These techniques are equally important in treating drug addiction.

Operant and Behavior Modification Techniques

Behavioral modification techniques provide the teacher or counselor with strategies for assisting young African-American males in performing desirable and appropriate behaviors, as well as promoting socially acceptable behaviors. It is a method to modify behavior to the extent that when a behavior is emitted in a variety of situations, it becomes consistently more appropriate.

Some cautions have been mentioned for teachers and counselors using behavioral strategies. The chief purpose of using this technique is to change or modify behaviors. The teacher or counselor is not generally concerned with the cause of the behaviors, rather with observing and recording overt behaviors. These behavioral responses may be measured and quantified in any attempt to explain behaviors. There are occasions, however, when motivation and the dynamic causes of the behaviors are primary concerns for the teacher or counselor.

In spite of the cautions involving using behavioral modification techniques, most of the research supports its use (Salend & Whittaker, 1992; Lane & McWhirter, 1992; Rizzo & Zabel, 1988; Katz, 1991; Taylor, 1992). The major concerns voiced were that the technique must be systematically employed, the environmental constraints must be considered, and teachers, educators, counselors, and parents must be well versed in using the technique. This is especially true when used with drug addicts.

There are many ways in which behavior can be modified. Contingency contracting, peer mediation, task-centered approach, coaching, cueing, social-cognitive approaches, modeling, role playing, cooperative learning, special group activities, and skill streaming and cognitive behavior modification are to name but a few techniques to employ in reducing the drug intake of young African-American males.

Contingency Contraction. This technique involves pupils in planning and executing contracts. Gradually, pupils take over record-keeping, analyze their own behavior, and even suggest the timing for cessation of contracts. Micro-contracts are made with the pupil in which he/she agrees to execute some amount of low-probability behavior (Premack Principle) for a specified time. An example may be an individual who likes to play sports will be denied the opportunity to play until homework assignments have been completed.

Peer Mediation Strategies. Peer mediation strategies have been successfully employed to manage behavior. The model is student driven and enables students to make decisions about issues and conflicts that have an impact upon their lives. The model requires that students exercise self-regulation strategies, which involves generating socially appropriate behavior in the absence of external control imposed by teachers or other authorities. To be effective, the concept must be practiced and frequently reinforced through role models and demonstrations of pro-social skills. A significant amount of drug usage may be attributed to peer pressure. This strategy promotes modeling appropriate behavior and denounces the use of drugs.

Several investigations have shown that negative behaviors and discipline problems decrease when this strategy is used. For example, increase in cooperative relationships and academic advisement often follows. Findings also show an increase in task behaviors (Salend & Whittaker, 1992; Lane & McWhirter, 1992). Using this strategy with young African-American males may assist them in internalizing appropriate behaviors.

Task-Centered Approach. The task-centered approach to learning is another way to modify behavior. Pupils may be experiencing difficulty because they cannot grasp certain social skills concepts. Behavioral problems may stem from the frustration of repeated failure, such as poor attention or the inability to work independently or in groups. This system provides children a highly structured learning environment. Elements in the task-centered approach may include activities to promote:

1. Attention-level tasks designed to gain and hold the pupil's attention.
2. Development of visual and auditory discrimination activities as needed.
3. Interpretation and reaction to social-level tasks emphasizing skills related to social interaction.
4. Imitation of social exchanges, the development of verbal and social courtesies, and group participation activities.

Coaching

Appropriate coaching techniques may be employed by teachers and counselors to develop social skills for young African-American males. Some of the commonly known techniques include (1) participation, (2) paying attention, (3) cooperation, (4) taking turns, (5) sharing, (6) communication, and (7) offering assistance and encouragement. These techniques are designed to make individuals cognizant of using alternative methods to solving problems; anticipating the consequences of their behaviors; and developing plans for successfully coping with problems.

Cueing

Cueing is employed to remind students to act appropriately just before the correct action is expected rather after an action is performed incorrectly. This technique is an excellent way of reminding students about prior standards and instruction. A major advantage is that it can be employed anywhere, using a variety of techniques such as glances, hand signals, pointing, nodding, or shaking the head, and holding up the hand, to name but a few.

Cueing can be utilized without interrupting the instructional program or planned activities. The technique assists in reducing negative practices and prevents students from performing inappropriate behaviors.

Successful implementation of this technique requires that students thoroughly understand the requirement, as well as recognize the specific cue. Otherwise, the result may be confused students, especially when they are held accountable for not responding appropriately to the intended cue.

Social-Cognitive Approach

These techniques are designed to instruct students and to help students maintain better control over their behaviors, deal more effectively with social matters through self-correction and problem solving. Self-monitoring or instruction involves verbal prompting by the student concerning his/her social behavior. Verbal prompting may be overt and covert.

Making Better Choices. This social-cognitive approach is designed to assist students in making better choices. Group lessons are developed around improving social skills. Specifically, lessons promote forethought before engaging in a behavior and to examine the consequences of the behavior. The major components of this program include the following cognitive sequence:

1. Stop (inhibit response)
2. Plan (behaviors leading to positive behaviors)
3. Do (follow plan and monitor behavior)
4. Check (evaluate the success of the plan)

These steps are practiced by the students and reinforced by the teacher and counselor. Various social skills are identified by the teacher for the student to practice. Progress reports are kept and assessed periodically by both teachers and students.

Modeling

Modeling assumes that an individual will imitate the behaviors displayed by others. The process is considered important because children acquire social skills through replicating behaviors demonstrated by others. Educators and adults may employ modeling techniques to change and influence behaviors by demonstrating appropriate skills to model. The impact and importance of this valuable technique is often overlooked by teachers, who frequently fail to assess the impact of their behaviors on children.

Modeling, if used appropriately, may influence or change behaviors more effectively than demonstration of behavior. Consequently, many young African-American males model drug behaviors they observe in their communities. This is premised upon the fact that once a behavior pattern is learned through imitation, it is maintained without employing positive reinforcement techniques. Teachers should be apprised and cognizant of the importance of modeling for promoting appropriate social skills. Additionally, they should be trained and exposed to various techniques to facilitate the process.

Children do not automatically imitate models they see. Several factors are involved (1) rapport established between teachers and children; (2) reinforcing consequences for demonstrating or not demonstrating the modeled behavior; and (3) determining the appropriate setting for modeling certain behaviors (Bandura, 1963).

Students should be taught how to show or demonstrate positive behaviors by observing others performing positive behaviors in structured situations. The techniques provides for the structured learning of appropriate behaviors through examples and demonstration by others. Internal or incidental modeling may occur at any time and modeling activities may be infused throughout the curriculum at random. However, a regular structured time or period of day is recommended in order to develop structure in a variety of social conditions. Teaching behavioral skills through modeling is best accomplished by beginning with impersonal situations that most students encounter, such as the correct way to show respect for others. Activities should be planned based upon the assessed needs of the class and be flexible enough to allow for changes when situations dictate. As students master the modeling process, additional behavioral problems may be emphasized (Taylor, 1997).

Videotape Modeling

Videotape modeling is an effective way to improve self-concept. Children may be encouraged to analyze classroom behavior and behaviors of addicts and patterns of interaction through reviewing videotapes. In this way, children can see the behaviors expected before they are exposed to them in various settings. Videotape modeling affords teachers the opportunity to reproduce the natural conditions of any behavior in the classroom setting. Consequently, videotape modeling may provide realistic training that can be transferred to real experiences inside and outside of the classroom.

For young African-American males, educators may employ this technique to help transfer modeling skills to real-life situations. It has been proven as an effective tool to teach pro-social skills to this group.

Black Male Volunteers' Program

In an effort to improve education among African-American males, some authorities advocate an increase in the presence of African-American male role models. This approach is designed to prevent the development of negative and inappropriate behaviors and drug usage in school and the community. It is felt that the African-American male teacher in the early grades can have a remarkable effect on the students, especially in the inner city where single-parent, female-headed households are commonplace. It is important that African-American males have the opportunity to be a part of an environment where an African-American male role model shows concern for young Black males. When this occurs, the African-American male child's self-esteem and academic achievement most likely will improve. Project 2000 and The Educational Opportunity Program have demonstrated the importance of involving Black male role models in educating young African-American males (Taylor, 1997).

Project 2000

Project 2000 was a program implemented by The Center for Educating African-American Males at Morgan State University for three Baltimore City Elementary Schools. Project 2000 was modeled after a successful role model program implemented in 1988 at Stanton Elementary School in Southeast Washington, DC.

Using a network of business, community, and civic leaders, the center recruited adult males, particularly African-Americans, to serve as teacher assistants for one-half day per week in the classroom of kindergarten through third grade students. The major objective was to prevent the development of negative attitudes toward the school environment and to promote high levels of academic advisement among African-American males in the early grades by providing them with adult role models in their daily school experience.

The Educational Opportunity Program (E.O.P.)

The position of Black males would do better if they were exposed to positive Black male role models was experimented with through this project, which was designed to assign selected males to serve as tutors to young Black males. Initial results show that the project had a significant impact on reducing aggressive and negative behaviors and on increasing achievement, attendances, and positive attitudes toward girls and female authorities (Gibbs, 1991).

Male volunteers were carefully screened and recruited from a variety of businesses and organizations in both the public and private sectors. Volunteers came from all occupational levels and pledged to spend one-half day per visit with the boys. Visits were planned in advance in order that the classroom teacher would have time to augment the instructional program. Volunteers performed many duties and tasks, such as accompanying the class of field trips, assisting with discipline problems, checking seatwork and homework, monitoring laboratories, tutoring in academic subjects, duplicating materials, and designing games and activities to promote social growth.

Holland's (1992) view of using Black male models support the aforementioned position. According to Holland, if Black men do not return to the schools to assist in educating Black males and identifying with them, we will lose them to a world of crime and dope. Additionally, he stated that Black male models exercise more control over young Black males because young Black males want their attention and approval.

The reader should exercise caution in using this strategy, and legal advice is recommended, as the strategy has been challenged as a violation of civil rights. As a compromise, some school districts are using male and female volunteers with both girls and boys in integrated classes.

The E.O.P. Program, facilitated by Nathaniel McFadden at Lake Clifton-Eastern Senior High School in Baltimore, Maryland was designed to improve the social and academic skills of African-American male students. The program's objectives were to keep students from dropping out of school and to inspire them to go to college (The Abell Report, 1991).

Programs such as these have proven effective in the African-American community. In the first group trained from 1986 to 1990, 51 participants graduated from high school; 6 more completed high school within the year 1991; 49 were admitted to college (The Abell Report, 1991).

Positive effects have been obtained in the Project 2000 Program as well. In an all-male first grade class in Baltimore City, school officials stated that they have seen dramatic improvements. Only 1 of the 20 students involved in the program was below grade level. Discipline problems almost disappeared and attendance improved significantly. These two programs have shown that young African-American males can significantly benefit from the guidance of African-American male role models (Brown, 1991; Stewart & England, 1989).

Young African-American males are in desperate need of African-American role models, especially male. According to Wright (1992) a significant percentage of Black boys are from single-parent homes, usually headed by a female. As a result, the child's early childhood is frequently dominated by females. Wright (1992) affirmed that these young boys need legitimate Black male role models in their lives.

Mancus (1992) postulated that the absence of positive role models in impoverished urban neighborhoods and the feminization of the African-American family are given as the primary justification for assigning Black male teachers to classes of African-American male students. Studies have indicated that primary students' perceptions of a school, teachers, and programs are influenced by gender (Sloan, 1992). It is predicted, therefore, that boys will be more likely to see themselves as academically competent, thus, more inclined to achieve, when they have Black male teachers. Also, they will be more likely to share authority and express nurturing behavior when they see male teachers doing so. This premise further supports the need for African-American males as teachers and role models.

Effects of Fatherless Households

Gaeddert (1992) noted that it is from other people's actions that we become familiar with society's demands and the rules we are expected to obey as we imitate or selectively respond to models during social learning. According to Gaeddert (1992), males and females generally choose same-sex models. Therefore, the absence of fathers is likely to have adverse effects on the young African-American male child. A Black child born today has only a one in five chance of growing up with two parents until the age of 16 (Ingrassia, 1993). Two out of three births to Black women under 35 are out of wedlock (Smith, 1993). In the inner city, at least 40% of Black children are raised in fatherless homes (Shades & Edwards, 1987).

In these fatherless homes, a child is more likely to live in poverty. The 1990 census figures show that 65% of the children of Black single mothers were poor (Ingrassia, 1993). As such, they are exposed to greater risk, educationally and socially. Additionally, they are not likely to be promoted with their peers and probably will drop out of school sooner

(Ingrassia, 1993). Mothers can be smothering, especially if her son is the only man in her life (Smith, 1993). Ingrassia (1993) noted that the boys in particular need male models. Without a father, who will help them define what it means to be a man? Fathers do things for their children that mothers often do not. Though there are obviously exceptions, fathers typically encourage independence and a sense of adventure, while mothers tend to be more nurturing and protective. It is men that teach boys how to be fathers.

Because of a lack of readily accessible models to positively influence young African-American males' development, North Carolina has developed a Black male role model program (1987) designed to provide male influence in the lives of young African-American males. Data from the project indicate that the project has had a significant impact upon the behaviors of Black males.

Without a father, young Black males learn many negative attitudes which may have adverse affects upon their lives. This often means gangs, from which the message is that "women are whores and handmaidens, not equals" (Ingrassia, 1993, 17-19). This kind of mentality has led to separation of the sexes among African-Americans. Having a male role model that can enlighten the young child's understanding may help deter this way of thinking. The presence of the African-American male can serve this purpose, as many children otherwise would not have the presence of a father figure that can provide the guidance and caring so many young African-American males need.

Lapoint (1992) concluded that African-American male adults must become new role models of empowerment and advocacy to our youth, for it we do not teach and show them that we care about the quality of their lives, how else will they learn how to care and take responsibility for themselves?

In the absence of a father or a Black role model, many young African-American males are influenced by their environments. They may succumb to environments that are filled with vices and illegal influences. These types of environments foster the following statistics:

1.   One out of every 22 at-risk Black American males will be killed by violent crime.
2.   Fifty-one percent of violent crimes in the United States is committed by at-risk Black youths.
3.   One out of every 6 at-risk Black males will be arrested by the time they reach 19 (Ingrassia, 1993; Lapoint, 1992).

4.   One out of 3 young Black males are somewhere in the Justice System (Thomas, 1995).

Black Teachers As Role Models

African-American male teachers are few in numbers. Ironically, this is in contrast to the increasing Black student enrollment in urban elementary and secondary schools (Wiley, 1991; Graham, 1987). Recent data show that with the dwindling minority teacher representation, it is possible that a minority student could complete the K-12 school experience without ever meeting a minority teacher (Rancifer, 1991). This is unfortunate for the African-American students, as they are in desperate need of African-American role models.   As mentioned, many Black students may have low aspirations for school work because they cannot see themselves in a tangible manner in the worthy professions, which includes teaching (Rancifer, 1991; Stewart & Meier, 1989).

Moreover, as the proportion of white teachers grows, role models that might encourage minority students to pursue careers in education decreases (Irvine, 1989). Without sufficient exposure to minority teachers throughout their education, both minority and majority students come to characterize the teaching profession, and the academic enterprise in general, as best suited for whites. The presence of the African-American role model is needed to address this mentality. In all too many instances, Black peers serve to lower academic achievement by labeling those who do well in school as "wanting to be white," and making it clear that Black boys can either be popular or smart but not both (Gill, 1991).

The continued presence of Black teachers and administrators in the schools, the maintenance of a climate supportive of ethnic pluralism, and the concept of multicultural education, all correlate with maximizing the opportunities for educational excellence for young African-American males. These professional adults are the "significant others" for young African-American males who act as appropriate role models and are capable of enhancing the boy's self-concept. They are particularly important in the lives of children who may otherwise lack daily contact with educated, intelligent, successful Black role models (Lapoint, 1992).

The presence of an African-American male teacher is especially important for these boys, as many of them are from single-parent, female-headed households. Their most significant role models from birth to age four or give have been female relatives (Holland, 1991). Also, the absence of a sturdy and contributing male parent in a major percentage of Black families denies the young African-American male a readily accessible model to positively influence his development (Wake County Public Schools, 1987)

McRae (1994) designed a study to determine if the perceptions of Black and white teachers supported the concept that Black American male teachers made a difference in establishing proper role models for Black boys, as well as positively impacting their self-concepts, social behavior, and academic performance. Thirty-nine educators were interviewed concerning their perceptions toward Black teachers as role models.

Two research questions were formulated to guide the research:

1.   Will African-American male teachers have a significant impact upon the self-concept of African-American male students?

2.   Does the presence of African-American male teachers in the classroom have a positive effect upon the academic achievement of African-American male students?

Sample. The sample was randomly selected from Baltimore City elementary teachers attending a local college and educators at an elementary school in the city. Prior permission had been given from the public schools to interview the participants. A total of 39 educators participated in the research project.

Instrument. An interview schedule was constructed and submitted to a panel of experts for validation. Based upon their input, the instrument was modified. The final revised instrument was used to interview participants.

Analysis of Data. All 39 participants completed the interview, yielding a 100% response rate. Of these participants, 30 (77%) were African-American: 8 males (21%) and 22 females (56%; White: 3 males (7.6%) and 5 females (12.85); and 1 (2.6%) Pacific-Islander. Years of experience were reported as: (a) 0-2 years, 7 (18%); 3-5 years, 7 (18%); 6-10 years, 8 (21%); 11-15 years, 2 (5%); 16-20 years, 7 (18%) ; 21-25 years, 4 (10%); 26 or more years, 4 (10%).

The titles of the educators varied. There were 16 (41%) "regular" teachers, 15 (38%) special educators, and one each (2.6%) master teacher, principal, social worker, speech pathologist, resource teacher, assistant principal, counselor, and psychologist.

Data from participants appeared to support the major research questions of this investigation.

Research Question #1:

1.   Will African-American male teachers have a significant impact upon the self-concept of African-American male students?

Seventy-two percent (72%) of the participants reported that they believed that their presence would significantly increase the boy's self-esteem. They further articulated that they believed that the boys would see them as caring professionals who could relate to them and encourage them to succeed as well as improve their socialization skills.

Research Question #2:

2.   Does the presence of African-American male teachers in the classroom have a positive effect upon the academic achievement of African-American male students?

Participants were in agreement with the research question. A significant percentage (64%) responded that African-American male students being taught by an African-American male teacher would show improvement in achievement. Additionally, they noted that by having an African-American male as a teacher would provide the African-American student with opportunity to see himself as an intelligent, contributing professional, with purpose and promise.

Discussion. Results of this study are in agreement with the majority of research in the field, that is, Black male teachers have a significant impact upon the self-concept and academic achievement of African-American males. Additionally, more African-American male teachers are needed to improve their academic and social skills.

Participants in this study also agreed with the preponderance of research on Black role models which indicates that the presence of an African-American male teacher is especially important for young inner-city boys, many of whom are from single-parent, female-headed households. Their most significant role models from birth to age four or five have been females. The absence of a sturdy and contributing male parent in a major percentage of Black families denies the young African-American male a readily accessible model to positively influence his development.

Many of the special group activities reviewed appear to have significantly impacted upon the social and academic development for young African-American males. The Black male role model program has many merits for educating Black males; however, the legal and civil rights dimensions must be fully explored before attempting such a program.

The Role of the School in a Behavioral Setting

A meaningful approach to dealing with negative behavior would be isolate the behavior and then quantify, record, and observe the number of acts involved. When this determination has been made, the teacher or counselor is equipped to undertake a course of action to change the negative behavior. Social skills training is the technique advocated. Analysis of the behavior, using the checklist included in Appendix C, may lead the teacher to pursue a course of action.

All children, including young African-American males, enter

school with a wide range of learning abilities, interests, motivation, personality, attitudes, cultural orientations, and social-economic status. These traits and abilities must be recognized and incorporated into the instructional program (Bankee & Obiakor, 1992).

Pupils also enter school with set behavioral styles. Frequently, these styles are inappropriate for the school. Several techniques are recommended to change inappropriate behaviors in the classroom:

- Raise the tolerance of the teacher. Teachers generally expect pupils to perform up to acceptable standards. Additionally, they often assume that pupils have been taught appropriate social skills at home. Whereas this may be true for most pupils, frequently it is not true for young African-American males. By recognizing causal factors, such as environment, culture, and values, the teacher's tolerance levels may be raised.

- Change teacher expectations for pupils. Pupils generally live up to teacher's expectations. Teachers should expect positive behaviors from children. To accomplish this goal, behaviors will sometimes have to be modeled. It is also recommended that individual time be allowed for certain pupils through interviews and individual conferences where the teacher honestly relates how the child's behavior is objectional.

- Analyze teacher's behavior toward a pupil. Pupils use of teacher's overt behavior as a mirror of their strength in the classroom. When a positive reflection is projected, the achievement level is increased. When the message is overtly or covertly negative, the pupil has nothing to support his/her efforts. For example, if there is little positive interaction between pupil and the teacher, the pupil may conclude that his/her behavior is not approved by the teacher. Because the pupil depends so heavily on the teacher's behavior for clues, it is crucial that the teacher objectively analyze his/her interaction with the pupils.

Role Playing

Role playing is an excellent technique for allowing children to act out both appropriate and inappropriate behaviors without embarrassment, or experiencing the consequences of their actions. It permits students to experience hypothetical conditions that may cause anxiety or emotional responses in ways that may enable them to better understand themselves. Once entrenched, these activities may be transferred to real-life experiences.

Role playing may assist students in learning appropriate social skills through developing appropriate models by observing and discussing alternative behavioral approaches. Role playing may be conducted in any type of classroom structure, level, or group size. It may be individually or group induced. Through appropriate observations and assessment procedures, areas of intervention may be identified for role-playing activities.

Role playing assists children in identifying and solving problems within a group context. It is also beneficial to shy students. It encourages their interactions with classmates without aversive consequences. As with most group activities, role playing must be structured. Activities should be designed to reduce, minimize, correct, or eliminate identified areas of deficits through the assessment process.

Gill (1991) listed the following advantages of role playing:

- Allows the student to express hidden feelings.
- Is student-centered and addresses the needs and concerns of the student.
- Permits the group to control the content and pace.
- Enables the student to empathize with others and understand their problems.
- Portrays generalized social problems and dynamics of group interaction, formal and informal.
- Gives more reality and immediacy to academic descriptive material (History, Geography, Social Skills, English).
- Enables the student to discuss private issues and problems.
- Provides an opportunity for nonarticulate students and emphasizes the importance of nonverbal and emotional responses.
- Gives practice in various types of behavior.

Disadvantages include:

- The teacher can lose control over what is learned and the order in which it is learned.
- Simplifications can mislead.
- It may dominate the learning experiences to the exclusion of solid theory and facts.
- It is dependent upon the personality, quality, and mix of the teacher and students.
- It may be seen as too entertaining and frivolous

Gill (1991) investigated the effects of role play, modeling, and videotape playback on the self-concept of elementary-school children, 13% of whom were African-Americans. The Piers-Harris Children's Self-

Concept Scale was employed on a pre/post-test basis. Intervention was for a six-month period. Data showed that the combination of role playing, modeling, and videotape playback had some effect upon various dimensions of self-concept.

Cooperative Learning

A basic definition of cooperative learning is "learning through the use of groups." Five basic elements of cooperative learning are:

- Positive interdependence.
- Individual accountability.
- Group processing.
- Small group/social skills.
- Face-to-face interaction.

A cooperative group is one in which two or more students work together toward a common goal in which every member of the group is included. Learning together in small groups has proven to provide a sense of responsibility and an understanding of the importance of cooperation among youngsters (Adams, 1990; Schultz, 1990). Children need to socialize and interact with each other. Among the best known cooperative structures are Jigsaw, Student Teams Achievement Divisions (STAD), Think-Pair-Share, Group Investigation, Circle of Learning, and Simple Structures.

Cooperative learning strategies have the power to transform classrooms by encouraging communities of caring, supportive students whose achievements improve and whose social skills grow (Kagan, 1990). Harnessing and directing the power of cooperative learning strategies present a challenge to the classroom teacher, however. Decisions about the content appropriateness of the structures, the necessary management routings, and the current social skill development of the learners call for special teacher preparation (Johnson, Johnson, & Holubec, 1988; Allen, 1990). For successful outcomes with students,
teachers also need the follow-up peer coaches, administrative support, parent understanding, and time to adapt to the strategies (Slavin, 1991).

While cooperative models replace individual seat work, they continue to require individual accountability. Thus, teachers who use cooperative learning structures recognize that it is important for students to both cooperate and compete.

To use a cooperative structure effectively, teachers need to make some preliminary decisions. According to Kagan (1989) the following questions should be asked:

- What kind of cognitive and academic development does it foster?
- What kind of social development does it foster?
- Where in the lesson plan (content) does it best fit?

Teachers also need to examine what conditions increase the effect of cooperative strategies. Positive interdependence, face-to-face (primitive) interaction, individual accountability, and group processing affect cooperative learning outcomes.

The benefits of cooperative learning appear to be reflected in the following:

- Academic gains, especially among minority and low-achieving students.
- Improved race relations among students in integrated classrooms.
- Improved social and affective development among students (Kagan, 1989; Johnson et al., 1988; Slavin, 1991).

Cooperative learning practices vary tremendously. The models can be complex to simple. Whatever their design, cooperative strategies include:

- A common goal.
- A structured task.
- A structured team.
- Clear roles.
- Designated time frame.
- Individual accountability.
- A structured process.

We need cooperative structures in our classrooms because many traditional socialization practices are absent. Not all students come to school with a social orientation, and students appear to master content more efficiently with these structures (Kagan, 1989). The preponderance of research indicates that cooperative learning strategies motivate students to care about each other and to share responsibility in completing tasks. (Refer to Appendix D for some Cooperative Learning Strategies to use in the classroom.)

Cooperative Learning vs. Peer Tutoring

It is frequently assumed by parents that cooperative learning is another aspect of peer tutoring, but there are many significant differences between cooperative learning and peer tutoring. In cooperative learning, everyone is responsible for learning and nobody is acting as a teacher or a tutor.

On the other hand, in peer tutoring, one child plays the role of the teacher and another that of student or tutor. Thus, the initial teaching does not come from a student, but from a teacher because all students are exposed to basic concepts in a group. The tutor already knows the subject and material and teaches it to a peer who needs individualized remedial help to master a specific skill. Those who grasp concepts quickly become the designated tutor. These students reinforce what they have just learned by explaining concepts and skills to teammates who need help (Slavin, 1991). Cooperative work puts a heterogeneous group of students together to share ideas and knowledge.

Special Group Activities

In a paper presented at the annual meeting of the American Education Research Association, Dorr-Bremme (1992) advanced some unique techniques for improving social identity in kindergarten and first grade. Students sat in groups and planned daily activities; these activities were videotaped. Analysis of the videotapes revealed several dimensions of social identity to be important, such as academic capability, maturity, talkativeness, independence, aggressiveness, ability to follow through, and leadership ability. The teacher responded to students individually and as circle participants, depending upon how the behavior was viewed.

Findings indicated that social identity was the combined responsibility of everyone in the classroom interacting to bring about the most positive social behavior. Interactions between individual students and the teacher were minimized.

Skillstreaming

Skillstreaming is a comprehensive social skill program developed by McGinnis and Goldstein (1984). Social skills are clustered in several categories with specific skills to be demonstrated to foster human interaction skills needed to perform appropriate social acts. Clear directions are provided for forming the skillstreaming groups, conducting group meetings, and specifying rules. Activities include modeling, role playing, feedback, and transfer training. Feedback received in the form of praise, encouragement, and constructive criticism is designed to reinforce correct performance of the skills.

Cognitive Behavior Modifications

These techniques focus on having individuals think about and internalize their feelings and behaviors before reacting. The process involves learning responses from the environment by listening, observing, and imitating others. Both cognition and language processes are mediated in solving problems and developing patterns of behaviors.

Cognitive behavioral strategies are designed to increase self-control of behavior through self-monitoring, self-evaluation, and self-reinforcement. The strategies assist children in internalizing their behaviors, comparing their behaviors against predetermined standards, and providing positive and negative feedback to themselves. Research findings indicate that there is a positive relationship between what individuals think about themselves and the types of behaviors they display (Rizzo & Zabel, 1988). This premise appears to be true for young African-American males as well. Matching the cognitive and affective process in designing learning experiences for the individuals appears to be realistic and achievable within the school.

Summary

Regarding drug crime, socioeconomic status, and African-Americans, research findings have shown that young African-American males of lower socioeconomic status are significantly more likely to be involved in drug crimes than other groups of African-Americans or perhaps even whites. However, this fact clearly indicate why lower class African-Americans in general are significantly more likely to be involved in drug crime than other groups. It could well be that, as a whole, the African-American lower class is not at all involved in drug crime with the exception of poor, urban, young, unemployed males.

Drug abuse by African-Americans who are poor, unemployed, and young are prone to be found in the inner cities, ghettos, and slums. They tend to be singled out for especially stern punishment. The following recommendations have been made by Maurer and Huling (1995) to reverse this trend: (1) revise national drug spending priorities to offer treatment to one million addicts who do not have access to treatment each year, (2) divert non-violent property offenders and minor drug offenders to alternatives to incarceration, and (3) eliminate mandatory sentencing and other sentencing policies that have had a disproportionate impact on women and minorities.

Most learning is social and is mediated by other people. Consequently, young African-American males, as well as all children, profit when working in groups. Individual and group activities have proven to be successful in teaching appropriate skills. Behavioral intervention techniques have proven to be equally successful.

Many individual and group experiences have been designed to promote social growth among and between children. One of the most promising of these is cooperative learning. Cooperative learning promotes:

- Positive interdependence
- Face-to-face interaction.

- Individual accountability.
- Interpersonal and small group skills.
- Group processing (Johnson & Johnson, 1990; Slavin & Oickle, 1981).

Most young African-American males do not attain academic success due partly to their inability to implement the proper social skills. These suggested techniques are designed to reduce student isolation and increase students' abilities appropriately to react and to work with other students toward the solution of common problems. Teachers should experiment with various forms of individual, group, and behavioral intervention strategies to improve the social skills of young African-American males (Taylor, 1992). Since most behaviors are learned, they can be changed through behavioral intervention. Once new social skills are learned through the application of these techniques, they become automatic (refer to chapter 4 for additional strategies).

Lutfiya (1991) outlined three strategies for successful group facilitation: (1) facilitation, (2) interpretation, and (3) accommodation. All three approaches depend upon cooperation within the group and roles are shared by all involved. Although this approach is primarily used to diagnose and evaluate disabled individuals, implications for group planning are clear.

Social skills interventions are needed if young African-American males are to be successfully integrated into the mainstream. Activities such as greeting, sharing, cooperating, assisting, complimenting, and inviting should be developed and modeled and infused throughout the curriculum (Anita & Kreimeyer, 1992).

Although the population of African-American children entering school is increasing, the available pool of African-American teachers is declining. This is unfortunate, as the literature has shown that African-American students are in desperate need of African-American role models, especially male.

The African-American child needs to see African-American males with whom they can identify and try to emulate by seeing their employment as worthy professions. They need to see African-American males as intelligent, capable, worthy, and contributing citizens. One of the best ways for this to occur is to have African-American male teachers in the classroom. African-American male teachers may be the only father figure for many urban African-American students since many come from single-parent, female-headed households. In many of these female-headed households, there are no male figures for the young child to positively identify with, such as uncles, grandfathers, or cousins.

The absence of fathers has been identified as contributing to the adverse conditions and, subsequently, the plight of the African-American male today. In the fatherless home, a child is more likely to live in poverty and is at greater risk educationally. Finally, the child is less likely to learn what it means to make and keep a commitment.

Without a male role model in these fatherless homes, the child may be influenced by the environment - environment that is often filled with gangs and individuals dealing in illegal activities. Without African-American male teachers and other positive Black role models, the boys may emulate the inappropriate models to which they have been exposed.

The presence of African-American male teachers, as well as other positive adult African-American male role models, has proven to be successful. The Project 2000 Program directed by Spencer Holland had already reported success. Similarly, the Educational Opportunity Program (E.O..P.) at the Lake Clifton-Eastern Senior High School in Baltimore, Maryland has also reported success by having African-American male teachers help combat the ills of African-American students' experience.

From these examples, it is evident that the presence of an African-American male teacher as a role model can be instrumental in improving the self-concept and academic achievement of the African-American male child. Several studies have employed the use of operant and behavior method to change drug intake (Rosenberg, 1979; Smart, 1974; O'Farrell & Feehan, 1999; Bigelow, Brooner, & Silverman, 1998; Horan, Rude, & Keillor, 1999; Newman & Ratto, 1999; Marlatt, 1973; Miller & Hedrick, 1999; Taylor, 1983).

These studies in general have claimed to be effective in treating various forms of alcoholism. Since they are frequently individualized, they may be called individualized behavior approaches to behaviorally control drug abuse by creating an environment for the client to role play a condition, whereby the young African-American males develop strategies to find solutions or alternative ways of reacting to the problem, other than taking drugs. The ultimate aim of the techniques is to have the client to employ self-control in drinking. These studies are premised upon the principle that drug abuse is learned operant behavior when positive reinforcement may significantly reduce drug usage.

Operant and behavioral models are designed to correct maladaptive behaviors. In the case of the drug addict, maladaptive social behaviors may be caused by the over usage of drugs. Strategies outlined in the   model are designed to change behavior through introducing reinforcement for limiting the intake of drugs. A variety of approaches are used   in behavioral intervention as articulated throughout this chapter.

Research findings have validated the use of these techniques to change maladaptive behavior in most social situations.

Chapter 6

Factors and Guidelines with a Social Skills Curriculum in Drug Education

Introduction

The increased addiction to hard drugs among young African-American males has alarmed many segments of our society. The common consensus is that the school should provide leadership to decrease this present trend. In response to the increase in drug abuse, as well as pressures from parents, the community, local, state, and federal officials, school districts have rapidly developed drug education programs on all grade levels (Goode, 1993; Brown, 1995). Intervention should start as early as the third grade, many young African-American males have been exposed to drugs by this time. It is felt that the school is the best source to provide a quality drug education program, since many children are exposed to its influence. To be charged with such a task, educators will have to plan systematically and comprehensively to develop quality programs that will reflect the many physical, social, and psychological problems faced by potential drug users as well as abusers.

What is needed are realistic and specific guidelines that can assist administrators in developing quality drug education programs. These guidelines should be designed to address all aspects of the drug problem, including promoting social and emotional growth and learning related to drug abuse, as well as providing information to construct a comprehensive drug education program stressing student, community, and specialist involvement (Ellickson, Bell, & McGuigan, 1993; Keller, & Dermatis, 1999; U. S. Department of Health and Human Services, 1993).

The voluminous amount of literature on drug abuse and drug education contains few experimental studies attesting to the effectiveness of drug education programs. Most of the research presents information relative to the legal, moral, and psychological; prevention, culture, and causes of drug addiction (Chassin, 1984; Shedler & Block, 1988). These studies have validated the need to use results from longitudinal and experimental studies to develop comprehensive drug education programs.

Development of comprehensive drug program is expensive. It was hoped that with the signing of the Comprehensive Drug-Control Bill by President Nixon on October 27, 1970, that school districts would have ample funds to develop comprehensive drug programs. Reasons why this Drug-Control Bill has done little to reduce drug usage, especially for young African-American males are highlighted throughout this chapter.

There are three popular programs currently in use which were developed to reduce drug intake among youth. They are Drug Awareness and Resistance Education (D.A.R.E.), Here's Looking At You, and McGruff's Drug Prevention and Child Protection. Studies have shown that there is no empirical evidence to show that D.A.R.E. programs, Looking At You, and the McGruff programs are effective in reducing drug abuse (Lynan & Bosworth, 1997; Elliott, 1995). These programs have not had any significant impact on drug reduction among youth, because they are not attuned with today's youth, including young African-American males (Brown, 1997; Brown, 1995; Brown, 1993).

In order for drug education programs to be effective they must recognize student's abilities to make decisions relative to drug education such as, differentiate between use and abuse (Rosenbaum, 1999; Brown, 1997). The authors articulated that curricula should be age specific, stressing student's participation and provide science-based objective educational materials. In addition, a realistic and functional drug education program must have community support and have an evaluation component to determine its effectiveness for young African-American males (Caligur, 1992, Dusenburg, Lake & Falco, 1997; Peele, 1996). The listed guidelines have been developed to assist administrators in developing a comprehensive drug education program.

Basic Factors to Consider in a Drug Education Program

Drug education programs involve several critical components, the first being to develop goals, objectives, and activities that emphasize people, not drugs. Secondly, since the school reaches a large population of youth, it is realistic to assume that a drug problem should be taught in the school by school personnel. Thirdly, involve students, let them discuss the subject. The drug program should include interactive strategies, such as individual and group discussions turned to the cultural and life styles of young African-American males, rather than didactic teaching adapted to the development level of the children. Fourthly, provide alternatives, instead of teaching that drugs have not provided the better life, show students that drugs are not needed to attain success in life. Fifthly, a drug education program must be varied and community wide and include opportunities for parents to reinforce drug information and concepts specific to the drug problem in the community (Beck & Mamola, 1989).

Development of Guidelines

To achieve the purposes of this chapter and to consider some basic factors needed in a drug education program several guidelines have been developed (Taylor, 1972). These guidelines are not exhaustive and should be considered as one of many approaches in developing quality drug education programs for young African-American males.

1. Drug education programs should begin at an early age. If the vicious drug cycle is to be checked, programs should begin early to orientate young African-American males about drugs and their potential effects. It is suggested that programs begin in the kindergarten and extend through grade twelve.

Recent drug education programs have dealt mostly with the senior high schools. Programs have extended downward to the elementary grades as well. During the developmental stages, customs, attitudes, opinions, and concepts are being molded by young African-American males' physical and social environment. It would appear that this would be an opportune time for the schools to capitalize on this learning opportunity.

An example of a drug education problem that includes the kindergarten through grade twelve might list the following indicators: (1) building self-esteem, (2) respecting the rights of others, (3) respecting individual differences, (4) learning methods of productive decision making, (5) learning information on the use and misuse of drugs, (6) reviewing information on health issues, and (7) learning how to make sound lifestyle choices. These indicators should be used on all grade levels, with experiences which are developmentally suited for young African-American males in various content areas (Refer to Chapters 5 and 6).

2. Students, parents, and community needs must be considered if drug education programs are to effectively serve the students. Instruments should be designed to elicit students, parental, and community attitudes and support towards the use of drugs, the danger of drugs, developing a drug education program, and participating in the program. Results should be used to develop construct a drug program based on the needs of the students, parents, and community. Students and community participation

can yield positive results that can invigorate the program content (O'Farrell & Fechan, 1999).

3. Clearly defined objectives should be written before any drug education program is initiated. Before an inservice training program is instituted, objectives should be determined. Objectives to a large extent will determine the program content. Objectives for inservice workshops should be broad enough to reflect changes in teachers' attitudes concerning various facets of drugs and drug abuse, improved interpersonal relationships with students through more sympathetic attitudes towards their problems, and involvement of parents and community personnel.

Objectives should be clearly stated in measurable terms so that the effectiveness of the program can be empirically evaluated at the end of the project. Workshop objectives as well as input from students and the community can aid in developing realistic objectives for the instructional aspect of the program. The nature of the instructional objectives will greatly depend upon the population to be served and special problems within a particular school district. The manner of organization and presentation of textual materials, audio-visual aids, students' activities, and testing materials should all emanate from the course objectives.

4. Intensive teacher and related school personnel education is essential for any successful drug education program. This is deemed important if teachers are to respond appropriately to students' impromptu questions concerning drugs and drug abuse. Exaggerated horror stories claiming that a diet pill may lead to heart failure, sterility, or insanity will not impress those who have seen local pill-heads alive and healthy on the streets. Much of the drug information heard by young African-American males is replete with myths, half-truths, old wives' tales, and gross misinformation regarding the effects of various kinds of drugs.

A realistic program for teachers should be developed. Workshops designed for one or two days cannot adequately cover the wide gamut of the drug problem and will leave little room for innovation. What is needed is an intensive program that extends a week or longer, as well as college based instruction given for credits.

An interdisciplinary approach should be evident for inservice workshops and college based instructional courses, with many specialists included to cover the wide spectrum of illegal, legal, moral, social, educational, physical, medical, and psychological factors inherent in the problem. A panel composed of a doctor, lawyer, school nurse, teacher, physical education instructor, clergyman, psychologist, and social worker should be presented to answer questions that might arise.

5. An instructional program for drug education should be based

on clearly defined objectives, needs of the students and community, and the availability of resources and qualified personnel. An instructional program must be as diversified as the causes that lead to drugs and drug abuse. A well rounded program is needed to dispel many of the myths about drugs, to decrease motivation that leads to drugs, and to give valid information concerning the illegal, legal, social, moral, medical, and psychological consequences of taking and using drugs (Schinke, Botvin, & Orlandi, 1991).

The general impact of an instructional program should be a preventive one to deter some pupils by giving them sufficient education and self-understanding concerning the act of drug usage, to encourage pupils already using drugs to realize their need for help, and to provide channels through which they can actively seek assistance (Newcomb & Bentler, 1998; Ponton, 1997).

It is evident that many students are already knowledgeable about the various effects of certain drugs and it is in part because of this knowledge that various drugs have become attractive and popular. Consequently, young African-American males responses and suggestions should be sought and used (Brown, 1997).

Students should be permitted to enter a drug education program on a non-compulsory basis. Small group sessions with no more than fifteen students appear to be the most effective for maximum group participation. The sessions should depend upon the needs and interest of the group involved. Skills in communicating with youths are also important, equally important are systems and schedules of evaluation of the programs' objectives (O'Connor & Saunder, 1992; Weiner, Prichard, 1993).

An instructional program for drug education should not be limited to one content area, but should be placed where the most students will receive maximum benefits even though more than one content area might be involved. The individual make-up of the school, personnel, and resources will largely determine the content area in which a drug education program should operate.

6. An interdisciplinary approach is needed to meet the many physical, psychological, and social problems inherent in drug education and abuse. Specialists in various fields should be invited to support the teachers' instructions. Specialists can also distinguish the difference between drug usage and abuse from their professional viewpoints and assist in changing attitudes towards drugs (Tucker, Donovan, & Marlatt, 1999; Higgins & Silverman, 1999). It is important for teachers and students to recognize that most substances have abuse potential - salt,

sugar, aspirin, and most medicines; and practically all drugs can be a source of abuse if not taken under controlled conditions. Again, specialists in various fields can render their expertise. Specialists should be scheduled to visit the class on regular intervals, depending upon the age and interest of the group.

Some of the specialists invited to speak might include physicians, pharmacists, lawyers, clergymen, psychologists, social workers, and mental health specialists from local, state, or federal departments. School administrators should seek experts with ability and experience in their disciplines, as well as individuals who have ability to relate to youths.

7. To facilitate the instructional process teachers and other personnel responsible for drug education programs should have specialized training attuned to the needs and characteristics of the group.

At this point it is assumed that teachers chosen to participate in the instructional program have had intensive inservice training or college training in various aspects of drug education. If not they should not be included in the program. The teacher is the key person in any instructional program. His/her role is more than a vehicle of knowledge. He/she must be able to mold student attitudes and beliefs and create a type of rapport that will elicit students' respect and support. Thus, it is of prime importance that teachers be exposed to various viewpoints concerning the drug problem by experts in the field. Intensive teacher education is essential if teachers are to adequately respond to questions with assurance. Teachers need detailed information to sway young African-American males from turning to drugs.

Reactions to be the presence of a teacher in the room where a drug education program is held can be mixed. This will greatly depend upon the rapport and interpersonal relationship established, as well as the degree of professional training displayed by the teacher.

It is believed that teachers properly trained with a prepared teacher's handbook which defines the tasks or the instructional method, as well as clearly defined objectives based on the needs and interests of the students, can do much to change the students' apprehension. It is incumbent upon teachers to see that youths in our communities receive factual information about drugs, both use and misuse.

Students will listen more readily to other students than to faculty members on topics dealing with drugs; therefore, whatever educational program is developed would be more effective and generate more student enthusiasm if it were organized with the aid of students.

Although it is felt that young persons can contribute greatly to a drug education program, it is recommended that they, too, receive intensive inservice training under supervision of qualified personnel, be carefully chosen, and be given a complete medical examination before working with youths. It is also believed that they should work under the direct supervision of the teacher and together plan and instruct youngsters about drugs.

In order to determine the instructional needs about drugs, surveys should be conducted in school districts in an effort to determine something about their approach to drug education. An additional approach would be to survey the availability of materials and resources needed to effectively conduct a drug education program in a particular school district. Instructional materials should be adjusted to the needs and interests of the group involved in the program. The instructional classroom for the program should not be isolated or remote from the rest of the school. It should be located where it will not readily call attention to itself. Groups should be small for maximum participation and discussions. Finally, visual aid equipment should be readily available.

8. Facilities, equipment, supplies, and resources should be evident before an instructional program in drug education is instituted.

9. There should be a well-defined guidance program to assist drug users as well as potential users. Guidance, to be most effective, is a continuous process that should be instituted along with a drug education program. It will need to include both process and content in order to decrease potential drug users as well as informing youths ignorant about drugs. Again, the guidance approaches to drug education must be as diversified as the causes leading to drugs, depending on the needs of the young African-American males. At times many of the specialists listed in the instructional process might be called upon to render their services and support the teacher or the counselor.

Group experiences of all kinds are needed. Guidance should be geared to utilizing youth talents under group conditions as well as involving individual youths who have symptoms of drug usage. Guidance should comprise the total academic setting, including the typical student, the clean-cut student, or athlete, as well as the atypical student, the hippie, and the pseudohippie, to be effective. Guidance should be offered during the regular school hours as well as after school hours to meet the many needs of students.

10. Evaluation of a drug education program should be an ongoing process based upon measurable objectives of the instructional process. A few of the drug education programs reported in the literature attempted to evaluate the effectiveness of a drug education program (Tobler & Stratton, 1997; United States General Accounting Office, 1990,

1992, 1993; Weiner & Prichard, et al, 1993). Students and community people were given questionnaires at the end of the program to complete. There were no indications that a pre-criterion test was administered to determine drug knowledge or attitudes towards drugs and drug abuse. The success of these programs in terms of helping young people combat the drug problem cannot be fully realized until some initial assessment is made before youths enter a drug education program. It is almost impossible to determine whether one program is more effective, acceptable, and/or efficient than another because of the lack of adequate evaluation procedures.

The evaluation procedure should match the program's objectives and where the program is designed to make specific changes in youngsters, these changes should be the basis for evaluation. In order to determine the full impact of a drug education program, students, school, and community personnel attitudes and knowledge must be assessed. Some following factors seem noteworthy of mentioned:

a.   Assess prior attitudes and knowledge towards the drug problem.

b.   List the objectives of the program in measurable terms. These should be based upon students, school, and community input.

c.   List the methods of evaluation. Such instruments as objective tests, checklists, rating scales, attitudinal scales and questionnaires may be instituted. These instruments should be administered on a pre-post basis and directly associated with the program's objectives. Instruments used in evaluating drug education programs must reflect both objective results that have been standardized and subjective results which includes attitudes and opinions.

d.   Collection of data - some systematic approach should be evident for recording data from instruments used and characteristics of the subjects involved in the program. Data collected should reflect the objectives of the program. Other types of data not germane to the objectives are useless for evaluating the program.

Thus, the end product of evaluation should be reflected in behavioral changes shown by the students, that is what the student does after the program compared with what he did before he initially entered.

11. Curriculum planning and development should be the final goal of a drug education program. Results from the evaluation of an

instructional program in drug education should be one of the principal components used in developing a drug educational curriculum. This information should reflect needed changes or modifications. Information gained from the evaluation process should be based on empirical methods.

Equally important will be input from students, teachers, subject matter specialists, experts in various fields, and the community. It is not the intent of this chapter to develop procedures needed in planning a curriculum, but to point out a series of tasks that should be followed to implement a quality drug education program; the curriculum being the end product with provisions for changes as needed (Refer to chapter 9).

Summary

In summary, the need for a comprehensive drug education program in the schools is evident. Well-planned and carefully controlled programs are needed as well as empirical research to shed more light on the drug problems from all aspects, legal, illegal, social, moral, medical, and psychological.

Such research must be conducted in relationship with the traits and characteristics of young African-American males involved, elementary, junior high school, and senior high school, with emphasis on prevention, intervention, and treatment. The major consideration should be the achievement of better insight into these problems. From this should come constructive and practical aids that will enable administrators and other concerned personnel working with the drug problem to plan systematically and comprehensively to reduce drug usage by students. The end product of comprehensive planning should reflect a functional curriculum based on the needs and interests of students.

The use of the guidelines appears to be one avenue designed to provide a quality drug education program for our youths since services provided by the school, not only affect their academic achievement but the complete socialization process as well. The highest quality of conditions and services should be made available to decrease this social menace called "drug abuse."

An attempt was made to outline one approach that appears to offer how an effective program in drug education can be developed. The guidelines outlined can be used to assess programs underway, or aid in implementing the development of new drug education programs. The listed guidelines may be employed by school districts to develop a comprehensive drug education program designed to improve the social skills of young African-American males. An example of a curriculum to improve social skills of this population appears in chapter 9, with a section on drug education.

Chapter 7

Parental Roles in Social Skills Development

Introduction

Educators must experiment with innovative ways of involving parents in the school (Harry & McLaughlin, 1992). Over the last several decades, the school has had a difficult time in establishing effective partnerships with parents. Generally, teachers tend to have little interaction with parents. Involvement and interaction may be improved through reporting to parents, holding conferences at times that are conducive for parents to attend, seeking parental assistance in planning and participating in field trips, in serving as resource individuals, tutoring children, and assisting with small groups planning special events.

Much of the noninvolvement has occurred because of hostility or parental indifference toward the school. Many schools serving young African-American males consider their parents a nuisance, unproductive, uneducated, lacking social grace, and not well informed on education and social issues. The relationship is further strained when parents internalize the negative behaviors displayed by the school and come to view the school as a place where they are unaccepted and which has no interest in them as individuals. There must be a total shift in the paradigm. The school must accept these parents and provide training and assistance in desired areas to effectively involve them in the educational process. Parental involvement should become a prime goal for all schools (Marion, 1981).

Parents may stimulate the social growth and development of their children in various ways. Designing everyday situations for them to explore, providing activities to promote self-esteem and confidence, praising them frequently, providing support, and assisting in creating a healthy and safe environment are but a few positive activities needed for normal child development.

Social changes are constantly occurring in early childhood. During this rapid expanding period, children gain self-awareness and learn how to respond appropriately in different situations. Making sure that appropriate social models are provided is a responsibility of parents. Children who are products of stimulating and positive environments bring a sense of social maturity and independence to the learning environment. Research findings by Lareau (1987) and Delgado-Gaitan (1991) support the above premise.

Strong families give children an edge in school. Children who participate in family functions tend to perform better in school than those who do not. Strong family ties appear to improve children's self-image and confidence. The family is the cornerstone for success in life. Parent education appears to play a role in how well students perform in school.

Minority students as a group tend to score lower than white and Asian students in most achievement areas. Results showed that 38% of Hispanic students obtained high scores while only 16% of Black students obtained high scores. By comparison, 58% of white and Asian students earned higher scores.

Quality of family life appears to be another significant factor in all groups. Black students from intact families performed better than those who lived only with their mothers. For example, strong family ties appear to reduce some of the anxiety faced by disadvantaged children. Further, Black children from families who attended church also scored higher on tests (Hilliard, 1988; Lynch, 1987).

Creative and innovative ways to gain family involvement must be experimented with, especially for parents of young African-American males (Mansbach, 1993). Factors such as (1) diverse school experiences, (2) diverse economic and time constraints, and (3) diverse linguistic and cultural practices, all combine to inhibit parental involvements.

Diversity should be recognized as a strength, rather than a weakness. Parents need to feel that their cultural styles and language represent valued knowledge, and that this knowledge is needed and welcomed in the school. One recommended approach is to dialogue with parents in order to understand what they think can be done to improve involvement (Finders & Lewis, 1994).

Unless these strategies are adhered to, children's academic and social development will be impeded. The cooperation of school and home is needed if social skills training is to be effective. There is an urgent need to involve parents by making them aware of their important role as well as training them.   Parental involvement should be sought in developing activities to promote interpersonal relations, including the effects of drugs on social development.   Several guidelines have been developed for this purpose.

Parental Guidelines for Promoting Social Growth

Young African-American males, as well as other children, follow general developmental milestones in social skills.   This predictable sequence permits parents to work with their children where they are developmentally and to pattern the learning of social skills in a more structured manner. Several guidelines are offered to aid parents:

Guideline I.   Initially, all learning comes through the five senses. Early expenses should be provided with as many concrete examples as possible using the five senses. Children's self-awareness, discovery, and interests in their environments are enhanced.

Guideline II.   Children should be permitted and encouraged to use the "discovery process" as much as possible by experimenting with appropriate social behaviors. Children explore their social world by trying out new behaviors. The effects that these behaviors have on others - how you respond - help shape the direction children will take. Children usually increase social behaviors that are rewarded by positive attention.

Guideline III.   Behaviors are learned by imitating others in the environment. The child observes the action of others and imitates those actions, thus acquiring new skills. Repeating those actions eventually leads to using them in functional situations. As the child develops, he/she is usually eager to imitate the "big kid" ways of older brothers and sisters or other children. This is especially true when applied to parents and other significant adults. Parents must teach children to imitate only positive social behaviors.

Guideline IV.   Play provides an opportunity for children to learn many social skills.   The chief "business" of childhood is play   Children gradually learn the give and take of group play. Enjoying playing near other children comes before the ability to play cooperatively with others. As play skills progress, the child can practice many social roles and act out many social situations within the security of make-believe play.

Guideline V.   Having friends is an important part of childhood development. Many social skills are learned such as sharing, taking turns, being a leader and follower, and   respecting the rights of others. As children develop, they need the companionship of other people. Follow the child's preference in selecting friends and provide opportunities for frequent play experiences at home and in the neighborhood. As children develop, being accepted and liked by other children becomes increasingly important. Learning to survive squabbles, hurt feelings, and changing affections is part of the normal but sometimes painful process of making friends.

Guideline VI. Praise your child frequently for successful completion of tasks. Provide social activities that ensure success. Set up the social situation for the child to be successful and show your pleasure through hugs, smiles, and perhaps special treats. Step in to help if your child is frustrated and on the brink of failure. Reward the child with plenty of praise for accomplishing what he/she was able to do and having the courage to attempt the rest.

Guideline VII. Provide activities to promote social decision making. Support the child in his/her decision making. Demonstrate alternate ways of arriving at appropriate decisions. As your child begins to signal definite opinions about his/her world, you can help practice making appropriate decisions, whenever possible, offer two acceptable choices and let your child make the decision; for example, "Do you want to play inside or outside today?" "Do you want to wear your baseball shirt or your PTA shirt to school?" or "How should you have done this another ways?"

Guideline VIII. Teach your child to respect ownership by recognizing others' possessions and property. Gaining a sense of "mine" makes a developmental step in self-awareness. As your child shows a preference for certain objects, make sure that he/she has ready access to these favorites, if appropriate. Talk about things and people in terms of what belongs to the child and what belongs to others (e.g., his/her shoes, his/her brother's shoes). Your child may also appreciate a special place within the home to use as a quiet play area and a secure space for treasured possessions.

Guideline IX. Demonstrate appropriate social behaviors in a variety of situations and have children to copy and model appropriate behaviors. Knowing "how to act" in different social situations is not easy for young children. By giving your child clear guidelines for good behavior, rewarding efforts, and giving opportunities to practice, the child will learn patterns of acceptable social skills. For example, practicing a quiet voice or whisper in make-believe play prepares your child for appropriate quiet manners in the library. Acting out the giving of presents can be a rehearsal for a first away-from-home birthday party. Model and teach good manners. Your child will learn from a wide variety of ordinary social experiences, such as going shopping, eating at restaurants, playing in the parks, and visiting friends and relatives. Do not expect your child's social behavior to be perfect. All children lapse into less mature behavior, especially when they are tired, frustrated, or in unfamiliar situations. Do not let the occasional embarrassment of a loud temper tantrum in a crowded shopping mall discourage you. Try to evaluate your child's behavior objectively, noting the successes as well as the problems.

Guideline X. Employ a variety of community resources to promote social experiences through direct participation by the child. Participating in community activities is one way your child can have fun while gaining social experiences with peers. Many communities offer a variety of activities designed to build social skills such as:

·   Preschool story hour at the library
·   Water play and swimming lessons
·   Children's films
·   Holiday parades
·   Holiday parties
·   Supervised play at "tot lots"
·   Dance classes
·   Children's exhibits at museums
·   Special events at shopping malls
·   Community outreach centers
·   Community fairs at neighborhood schools

Some Suggested Strategies for Facilitating the Social Learning Process
    The following are strategies for facilitating the social learning process of young African-American males, as well as children.

Relate Tasks to the Developmental Level. Some children are eager to start new tasks and experiences. Others need to be coaxed and encouraged. Regardless of how your child approaches challenges, success is important for the development of self-concept. Direct your child toward challenges that he/she is developmentally ready for. Break down big tasks into smaller parts, for example, if your child wants to make a garden, break down the project into small but easy steps - digging, making holes, dropping seeds, covering them, and watering. Show him/her each step, but let your child do it for himself/herself. Give praise abundantly; avoid criticism whenever possible.

Build a Sense of Security and Trust. Given a loving and responsive home environment, your child will be able to establish a sense of self apart from the people and things about her/him. Patience, consistency, and loving discipline are acts of caring that support your child as she/he strives toward independence. Praise the child for tasks well done.

Be Sensitive to Your Child's Signals. As an individual, your child shows unique ways of responding to new people and new experiences. Although he/she may not be able to put his/her feelings into words, he/she may need reassurance when entering into unknown territory. Sometimes fearfulness and negative behaviors are signs that your child is not quite ready for the challenge at hand.

Make Your Child and Equal in the Family. Membership in a family involves learning to share: sharing time, sharing material resources, sharing one another's love. As your child grows more capable, he/she should be given the opportunity to perform tasks that contribute to the functioning of the family. Your child also needs to be shown ways to express how much he/she cares about the people he/she loves.

Provide a Good Role Model for Your Child to Emulate. Practice makes perfect. Demonstrate appropriate role models for your child to follow. Children quickly remember what they see.

Be Aware of Your Child's Limitations. Realize that your child's present social capabilities are largely determined by his/her overall developmental level. Your expectations of social behavior should be based on developmental age, not chronological age. Set appropriate and realistic goals based upon the development pattern of your child.

Go From the Known to the Unknown. Prepare your child for new experiences by linking the familiar to the unknown. If your child has met the librarian and visited the children's room in the neighborhood library many times, then participating in preschool story hour is not so scary a prospect.

Summary

From the very beginning, your child has an important place within your family. By being responsive to your child's needs for comfort, play, and love, you build a foundation for positive interactive social relationships. The drive for independence emerges as developmental skills grow. As your child tries to do more and more for himself/herself, he/she continues to depend on you for guidance and support. Parent delight in the small accomplishments of a child can set expectations for 'larger successes.

Parents of young African-American males, as well as all parents, have a tremendous influence and impact through appropriate models for developing social skills. The developmental level of the child as well as the developmental sequence must be considered in social skills training.

In order for parents of young African-American males to be effective change agents in promoting appropriate social skills development, early intervention in healthcare, counseling, housing, nutrition, education, and child rearing practices, etc., must be improved. Early intervention and parental involvements are essential for preparing children to master social skill tasks successfully.

When necessary, the school should assume the responsibility of teaching parents how to provide their children with enriched experiences that will provide the necessary foundation for success in school. This approach minimizes failure and promotes positive self-concepts in young African-American males, as well as all children. At-risk young African-American males may lack the necessary experience to be successful in school. Parental training will assist in closing the learning gap.

There has been strong support from the federal government to include the family in the early educational process of their children. For example, the federal government has created guidelines for the educational community to use in developing and implementing a comprehensive, coordinated, multidisciplinary, interagency program of early intervention services for infants, toddlers, and their families (Gallager, 1989).

According to much of the research in the field, the role of parental participation in educating young African-American males has been limited. This view has been interpreted to imply that parents had no interest in the education of their children (Lynch & Stein, 1987; Marion, 1981). Several factors may contribute to the lack of parental participation and involvement. Many parents do not feel welcome in the schools, believing that they have little to offer in educating their children. Further, Cassidy (1988) reported that problems with scheduling, transportation, and knowledge of the instructional programs are partly responsible for poor parental participation.

Parents must feel that they are welcome in the school and be given responsibilities concerned with planning, collaborating with teachers, and policy-making. Parents should have an active role in planning and instructing their children and function as advocates for them if children are to profit significantly from their school experiences.

All persons benefit when an effective working relationship and rapport have been established. Parents should be informed on a regular basis of their children's progress in school. Schools should experiment with various ways of improving parental participation, since they are the foremost educators of their children.*

Chapter 8

Overview: Evaluating Social Skills of Young African-American Males

The relationship between social learning theories and the learning and academic performance of young African-American males is not well established. Most research reported today involves intervention for Black adolescents and youth males. It is necessary, therefore, to conduct empirical studies to determine to what degree social learning theories and early intervention impact the academic performance of young African-American males.

Taylor (1994) designed three experimental studies to test some of the constructs outlined earlier related to social skills development. Boys from grades 1 and 2 were selected to participate. Experiment #1 assessed the impact of a structured social skills program on academic and interpersonal skills, attendance, and office referrals. Experiment #2 was designed to determine the impact of a structured social skills program on reading a mathematics achievement of boys in grades 1 and 2. Finally, Experiment #3 assessed parents' and teachers' perceptions of the effect of the structured social skills program on the reading, mathematics, and interpersonal skills of boys in the first three grades.

Experiment #1

Subjects in this study were young African-American boys from a large metropolitan city in the east. Significant improvements were noted in social skills and academic performance along with positive changes in the boys' attitudes toward girls. Hypotheses were constructed to determine whether significant differences existed in reading, mathematics, interpersonal skills, attendance, fewer referrals to the office, and parents' and teachers' perception of social skills development. Major and minor hypotheses were tested. Significant levels were set at the .05 level of confidence.

Major Hypothesis

There will be a significant difference in the academic and interpersonal skills of African-American males after they have participated in a year-long structured program in social skills development.

Minor Hypothesis

1. There will be a significant difference in reading and math grades of African-American males after they have participated in a structured social skills program.

2. There will be a significant difference in the attendance and referrals to the office of African-American males after they have participated in a structured social skills program.

3. There will be a significant difference in the way parents and teachers perceive the social skills development of African-American males after participation in the structured social skills program.

Sample

Boys selected to participate in this study were enrolled in grades 1 and 2. The boys were administered a preassessment inventory before the intervention program which was initiated by teachers participating in the study. The inventory was not administered to determine who would be selected or rejected to participate. Rather, it was determine the types of social skills development that the boys needed (refer to Appendix B).

Instrumentation

A preassessment inventory was constructed and administered to African-American males who participated in the study. Results from the inventory indicated a variety of social skills deficits such as poor interpersonal skills, stress, poor organization and study skills, and destructive and aggressive behaviors. These deficits formed the basis for developing the structured social skills program and for grouping the boys into various groups for remediating or eliminating the social skills deficits.

A study assessment profile was constructed for teachers to record the boys reading and mathematics grades and social development on a pre/post-test basis. A social skills checklist was also developed and administered to the boys on a pre/post-test basis by teachers and parents. Forty items in the checklist were rated on a four-point scale ranging from always (a lot, sometimes) to never. Total scores were computed by teachers and parents for each boy involved in the study.

Intervention

Young African-American males who participated in this study were exposed to a year of structured social skills training. Activities included techniques for improving bonding, attention, belonging, recognition of their roles and positions in a group, developing confidence, motivation, caring, problem-solving techniques, and other behavioral problems.

For each skill a set of steps was developed and presented following a set sequence: (1) The teacher modeled the behavior; (2) the student attempted to repeat the demonstrated behavior; (3) other students critiqued the behavior; and (4) the student practiced the skill independent of the group. These steps assisted young Black males in internalizing their behaviors and assessing how their behaviors impact others.

The structured social skills program followed the listed format for each behavior taught:

1. Behaviors were written in behavioral terms.
2. Task analysis were applied until each skill was mastered before moving to the next skill.
3. Some physical arrangements in the classroom were necessary to accomplish some of the skills.
4. No specific time of the school day was devoted to skill training; rather, the training was infused into the regular curriculum whenever possible.
5. A reinforcement system was developed before the intervention was initiated.
6. Specific rules were developed for each skill with as much input from the boys as possible and written in observable and measurable terms.
7. Rules were understood by the boys; that is, they were able to complete the task.

In selecting skills, emphasis was placed on meeting the personal and social needs of the boys as perceived by them. Once the skills were selected, they were broken down into small manageable tasks (task analysis). New social skills were added only when students had successfully transferred a prior skill.

Analysis of Data

Data were recorded on a student assessment profile. Sum totals for each of the measures in reading, math, attendance, office referrals, and social skills development were used in analyzing the data. Several types of analyses were conducted, including descriptive statistics, "t" tests, and Kolmongorow-Smirnow test. Results for all measures were significant beyond the .01 level of confidence. Table 8.1 shows the number of absences between the two testing periods.

Table 8.1 Pre-Post Frequency Analysis of Days Absent (N=33)

No. of Days	No. of Persons Pre-test	Percent Persons Pre-test	No of Persons Post-test	Percent Persons Post-test
00	6	18	11	33
01	4	12	4	12
02	3	9	3	9
03	5	15.5	5	15.5
04	5	15.5	3	9
05	4	12	3	9
09	3	9	1	3
10	1	3	2	6.5
11	1	3	1	3
13	0	0	0	0
16	1	3	0	0
20	0	1	0	0
Total:	33	100%	33	100%

It is evident from Table 8.1 that the structured social skills training program had a significant impact on attendance. Perfect attendance increased from 18% to 33% by the end of the year. Generally, the boys showed a greater decrease in the number of days absent between the two recording periods. It should also be noted that there was a significant decrease in the number of lower days absent (13-20) between pre-and post-recordings.

The number of office referrals between the two recording periods are summarized in Table 8.2.

Table 8.2 Number and Percent of Office Referrals (N–32)

No. of Referrals	Pre- Number	Pre- Percent	Post Number	Post Percent
0	29	90.5	31	97
1	2	6.5	1	3
2	1	3.0	0	0
Total:	32	100%	32	100%

Table 8.2 shows the number of referrals between the two recording periods. Some differences can be seen between the number of referrals between the two periods. There was a significant decrease in office referrals between the two periods. During the post-period, 31 (97%) of the boys were not referred to the office compared to 29 (90.5%) during the pre-period No boys were referred during the post-period more than twice.

Results

Table 8.3 outlines the numbers and percentages of pre/post reading and mathematics grades of young African-American males participating in the study.

Table 8.3 Frequency Analyses of Pre-Post Reading and Mathematics Grades (N=33)

	Reading				Mathematics			
	Pre-	Pre-	Post-	Post-	Pre-	Pre-	Post-	Post-
Grade	#	%	#	%	#	%	#	%
Good	8	24	13	39	1	3	10	30
Satisfac.	14	42	18	54	12	36	14	42
Unsatis..	5	15	1	3.5	5	15	6	19
Fail	6	19	1	3.5	12	46	3	9
Total:	33	100	33	100	30	100	33	100

Table 8.3 reveals that grades in reading and mathematics improved significantly between the two testing periods. Specifically, there was a significant increase in "Good" grades for both subjects. The satisfactory categories showed the greatest gains. The unsatisfactory category showed a slight decrease for each measure; similarly, a decrease

was noted in the number of failing grades received between the two testing periods.
Chi-square results are reported in Table 8.4 for reading and mathematics achievement.

Table 8.4 Chi-Square Values Pre/Post Achievement Reading and Mathematics (N=33)

	X2	P
Reading	19.8	>.001
Math	12.8	>.001

Both reading and mathematics achievement showed a significant difference between the pre-and post-testing periods. Both measures were significant beyond the .001 level. These results imply that the intervention had a positive effect on the reading and mathematics achievement of young African-American males.

Table 8.5 shows the means, standard deviation, and "t" test results for reading and mathematics achievement.

Table 8.5 Means, Standard Deviations, and T-Test Analyses For Reading and Mathematics Grades

Measures	Pre-Analyses Mean	SD	Post-Analysis Mean	SD	T-Value	P
Reading	3.85	1.004	4.49	1.176	5.60	>.001
Math	2.758	1.323	4.121	1.193	7.22	>.001

Inspection of Tables 8.4 and 8.5 clearly shows that significant differences occurred between the two testing periods in reading and mathematics achievement. The significant level surpassed the .001 level of confidence. These data suggest that the structured social skills program had a significant impact on the reading and mathematics achievement of the young African-American males. Thus, the hypothesis stating that there will be a significant difference in reading and mathematics achievement of African-American males after they had participated in a structured social skills program was supported beyond the .001 level of confidence.

Pre/post perception of the social skills development of the boys participating in the study as viewed by parents and teachers in reflected in Table 8.6 and Table 8.7.

Table 8.6 Teachers' Perception of Social Skills Development (N=28)

PRE-SOCIAL SKILLS		POST -SOCIAL SKILLS	
SCORE	NUMBER	SCORE	NUMBER
-48	1	13	1
-59	1	13	1
-65	1	14	1
-67	1	15	1
-68	1	17	1
-75	1	18	1
-76	2	18	1
-77	1	20	1
-78	3	21	1
-79	2	21	1
-81	1	21	1
-83	1	23	1
-85	1	24	1
-88	1	24	1
-91	3	25	4
-92	1	28	1
-93	1	28	1
-95	2	28	1
-97	1	29	2
-100	1	30	1
-106	1	31	4
Total:	**28**	**Total:**	**28**

Table 8.7 Parents' Perception of Social Skills Development (N=21)

PRE-SOCIAL SKILLS SCORE	NUMBER	POST-SOCIAL SKILLS SCORE	NUMBER
-67	1	31	2
-74	1	29	1
-79	2	28	3
-82	1	27	1
-84	1	26	3
-85	2	25	3
-88	3	23	1
-89	1	24	1
-90	1	22	1
-91	1	21	2
-92	2	20	2
-95	5	18	1
Total:	**21**	**Total:**	**21**

Data in Tables 8.6 and 8.7 strongly suggest significant differences in social skills development as reported by both teachers and parents. Teachers tended to rate social behavior growth higher. Results supported the hypothesis stating that parents and teachers would perceive social skills development of African-American males as positive after they had participated in structured social skills.

The Kolmogorow-Smirnow Statistical Test was used to analyze the impact of the intervention on absences and office referrals. Data are shown in Table 8.8.

Table 8.8 Means, Standard Deviations, and Kolmogorow-Smirnow (K-S) Analysis for Absences and Office Referrals (N=33)

	Pre-Measure K-S				Post-Measure K-S			
Measure	Mean	SD	Value	P	Mean	SD	Value	P
Absences	5.121	4.827	0.994	>.01	3.667	5.206	1.552	>.01
Office Referrals	0.281	0.883	2.933	>.01	0.094	0.296	3.086	>.01

The results shown in Table 8.8 support the hypothesis stating that there would be a significant difference in attendance and office referrals of African-American males after they had participated in a structured social skills program. All of the measures were significant beyond the .01 level of confidence.

Perceptions of social skills development as reported by teachers and parents are reflected in Table 8.9

Table 8.9 Means, Standard Deviations, and Kolmogorow-Smirnow Analysis of Social Skills Development (N=33)

	Pre-Social Skills K-S				Post-Social Skills K-S			
Social Skills	Means	SD	Value	P	Means	SD	Value	P
Parent	87.048	7.553	0.8111	>.01	24.952	3.653	0.592	>.01
Teacher	81.821	13.024	0.6566	>.01	23.500	5.840	0.7633	>.01

Data in Table 8.9 strongly suggest significant differences in the social skills development as reported by teachers and parents. Significant differences beyond the .01 level were reported for both groups (teacher and parents). Data supported one of the listed hypotheses, which stated that parents and teachers would perceive social skills development of

African-American males as positive after they had participated in a structured social skills program.

Significant differences reported in Tables 8.8 and 8.9 strongly supported the major hypothesis of this study; that there would be a significant difference in the academic and interpersonal skills of African-American males after they had participated in a year-long structured program in social skills development. All measures were significant beyond the .01 level of confidence.

Discussion

Generally, most of the African-American males in this study were pleased with their progress and voiced an interest in continuing with the program. Similarly, both teachers and parents were pleased with the significant social and academic gains that students had made in improving their academic and interpersonal skills.

The findings of this investigation imply that there is a vital need to intervene and teach social skills to African-American males at an early age. Thus, the data tended to support the premise that deficits in social skills development can be compensated for African-American males if early systematic planning is conducted involving both the home and the school.

Recommendations

The project appeared to have changed some of the boys' negative and aggressive behavior, enhanced their self-images, and increased achievement in reading and mathematics. The following recommendations would strengthen the program:

1.   The total resources of the school should be used and integrated in order to bring about desired changes in behavior.

2.   Additional studies should be attempted in other schools to see if the results of this study can be replicated.

3.   Parents must become an integral part of all planning designed to improve the social skills of their children.

4.   Studies should be designed to follow up on the progress of the project for the boys over a span of three to four years to determine the long-term effect of the structured social skills program on behavior.

Experiment #2

The study was designed to employ social skills to improve reading and mathematic skills. A structured social skills program was developed for young African-American males in a large urban setting. Thirty-three boys were selected to participate in the study. The boys had previously demonstrated social skills deficits as determined by a preassessment instrument.

The structured social skills program was conducted over a one-year period. Finding indicated that the boys showed significant improvement in interpersonal skills as well as reading and mathematic achievement. All measures were significant at the .01 level or greater; specific recommendations were made for strengthening the program.

Major Hypothesis

There will be a significant difference in the reading, mathematics, and interpersonal skills of young African-American males as viewed by teachers and parents after they have participated in a year-long structured program in social skills development.

Minor Hypothesis

1. There will be a significant relationship in the reading and math achievement of young African-American males as perceived by teachers and parents after they have participated in a structured social skills program.

2. There will be a significant relationship in how parents and teachers perceive the social skills development of young African-American males after they have participated in a structured interpersonal program.

Sample

As in Experiment #1, boys selected to participate in this study were in grades 1 and 2; teachers and parents of these boys (N=28 for both groups) also participated.

Instrumentation

A Likert-type scale was constructed and administered to the teachers and parents on a pre/post-test basis relevant to mathematics, reading, and interpersonal skills. There were 36 items in the instrument, which were rated on a five-point scale ranging from strongly, agree to strongly disagree. Total scores were computed.

Intervention

Young African-American males who participated in this study were exposed to a year of structured interpersonal and social skills strategies. The program was designed to determine if social skills training has any impact upon mathematics and reading performance.

The same steps employed for social skills training in Experiment #1 were used in Experiment #2: (1) The teacher modeled the behavior; (2) the student attempted to repeat the demonstrated behavior; (3) other students critiqued the behavior; and (4) the student practiced the skill independent of the group. These steps assisted young Black males in internalizing their behaviors and assessing how their behavior impacted others.

The structured social skills program followed the listed format for each behavior taught:

1. Behaviors were written in behavioral terms.
2. Task analysis was applied until each skill was mastered before moving to the next skill.
3. Some physical arrangements in the classroom were necessary to accomplish some of the skills.
4. No specific time of the school day was devoted to skill training; rather, the training was infused into the regular curriculum whenever possible.
5. A reinforcement system was developed before the intervention was initiated.
6. Specific rules were developed for each skill with as much input from the boys as possible, and written in observable and measurable terms.
7. Rules were understood by the boys; that is, they were able to complete the task.

New social skills were added only when students had successfully transferred a prior skill.

Mathematics and reading instruction followed the prescribed curriculum. No special technique or innovative strategies were used. The intent of the study was to determine the effects of a structured social skills program on mathematics and reading achievement.

Analysis of Data

Sum totals for each of the measures in reading, math, and social skills development were used in analyzing the data. Several types of analyses were conducted, including Chi-squares and correlations. The Chi-square results were computed for reading and mathematical achievement as well as social skills development to determine significant levels. Significant levels were set at the .05 level of confidence for all measures. Correlations were computed to show the relationship between the variables on a pre/post-test basis.

Table 8.10 shows how teachers and parents perceived the impact of a structured social skills program on social skills, mathematics, and reading skills.

Table 8.10 Chi-Square Results of Parents' and Teachers' Perceptions of the Impact of the Social Skills Program on Mathematics and Reading Achievement (N=33)

VARIABLES	X^2	P
Social Skills	3.92	>.05
Mathematics	4.44	>.05
Reading	5.39	>.05

Data in Table 8.10 clearly show that parents and teachers thought that the structured program in social skills significantly affected the reading, mathematics, and social skills of the boys involved in the study. All measures for the study variable were greater than the .05 level of confidence. Chi-square results supported the major hypothesis of this study, which stated that there will be a significant difference in the reading, mathematics, and interpersonal skills of young African-American males as viewed by teachers and parents after they have participated in a structured social skills program.

Table 8.11 summarizes the correlations of teachers' and parents' view of the study's variables.

Table 8.11 Correlations of Teachers' and Parents' Perceptions of

Pre/Post-test Results Between Three Basic Study Variables (N=33)

VARIABLES	Teacher	Parent	Teacher	Parent	Teacher	Parent
Social Skills	.38	.24	.70	.23	.51	.22
Math	.63	.51	.74	.47	.76	.50
Reading	.83	.48	.79	.33	.81	.49

Correlations were computed to determine if significant relationship existed between the perceptions of teachers and parents toward the study variables. All variables correlated significantly. Data suggested that both parents and teachers agreed that the training program made a significant impact on the boys in the areas of reading, mathematics, and social skills development.

These data support the minor hypotheses of this study.

Hypothesis #1. There will be significant relationship in the reading and mathematics of young African-American males as perceived by teachers and parents after they have participated in a structured social skills program.

Hypothesis #2. There will be a significant relationship in how parents and teachers perceive the social skills development of young African-American males after they have participated in a structured interpersonal program.

Discussion

Thus, there were significant agreements among and between the groups relevant to the benefits of the program. Results of this study clearly showed that parents and teachers overwhelmingly viewed the structured program in interpersonal skills as highly successful. Additionally, the program appeared to have improved communication between the teachers and parents. They worked cooperatively for the benefit of the boys. For example, a significant number of parents volunteered to work in the structured program.

Not only did the boys show significant improvement in reading and mathematics, they also showed significant improvement in social skills. Near the conclusion of the program, boys were observed using appropriate manners, following school and classroom rules, coming to

school on time, being less tardy, and showing respect for girls and adult authorities.

Recommendations

Both teachers and parents gave high praise for the program and recommended that it become part of the regular curriculum. Specific recommendations include:

1. Parents should be encouraged to participate frequently in school activities.
2. Additional activities of this nature should be jointly planned by teachers and parents.
3. Parents should be given specific information relevant to improving social skills.
4. Follow-up studies should be conducted over a span of years to determine the long-term effects of social training.

Experiment #3

Experiment #3 was designed to determine parents' and teachers' perceptions of the use of a structured social skills program to improve the reading, mathematics, and interpersonal achievement of young African-American males. The structured social skills program, as in Experiments #1 and #2, was conducted over a one-year period. Findings indicated that the boys showed significant improvement in reading, mathematics, and interpersonal skills.

Major Hypothesis

There will be a significant difference in the reading, mathematics and interpersonal skills of young African-American males after they have participated in a year-long structured program in social skills development.

Minor Hypothesis

1. There will be a significant difference in the reading and mathematics achievement of young African-American males after they have participated in a structured social skills program.
2. There will be a significant difference in the way parents and teachers perceive the social skills development of young African-American males after they have participated in a structured social skills program.

Method and Procedures

Method and procedures identical to those employed in Experiments #1 and #2 were used. The one exception was the grade level of the boys who participated. Thirty-three boys in three first grades were selected to participate.

Analysis of Data

Data were recorded on a student assessment profile. Sum totals for each of the measures in reading, mathematics, and social skills development were used in analyzing the data. Several types of analyses were conducted, including descriptive statistics and the "t" test. The "t" test results were computed for reading and mathematical grades as well as to determine significant levels on other measures. Significant levels were set at the .05 level of confidence for all measures.

Results

Table 8.12 outlines "t" test values of pre-post reading and mathematics grades of African-American males participating in the study.

Table 8.12 Means Standard Deviations, and T-Test Analyses for Reading and Mathematics Achievement

	Pre-Analysis		Post-Analysis		T-Value	P
Measure	Mean	SD	Mean	SD		
Reading	3.67	1.02	4.61	1.172	5.60	>.001
Math	2.56	1.321	4.13	1.193	7.22	>.001

Inspection of Table 8.12 clearly shows that significant differences occurred between the two periods (pre/post) in reading and mathematics achievement. The significant level surpassed the .001 level of confidence. Data suggest that the structured social skills program had a significant impact on the reading and mathematics achievement of the young African-American males. Thus, the hypothesis stating that there will be a significant difference in the reading and mathematics achievement of African-American males after they have participated in a structured social skills program was supported beyond the .001 level of confidence.

Pre/post perceptions of the social skills development of boys participating in the study as viewed by parents and teachers are reflected in Tables 8.13 and 8.14.

Table 8.13 Parents' Perception of Social Skills Development (N=21)

Pre-Social Skills		Post-Social Skills	
Score	Number	Score	Number
-69	1	30	3
-76	1	33	1
-82	2	34	4
-86	1	30	1
-80	1	31	1
-88	2	29	3
-93	3	25	1
-86	1	23	1
-95	1	20	1
-86	1	19	2
-93	2	18	2
-91	5	16	1
Total:	**21**	**Total:**	**21**

Table 8.14 Teachers' Perception of Social Skills Development
(N=28)

	Pre-Social Skills			Post-Social Skills	
	Score	Number		Score	Number
51	1		15	1	
	-61	1		12	1
	-63	1		11	1
	-65	1		16	1
	-62	1		19	1
	-77	1		21	1
	-74	2		19	1
	-78	1		21	1
	-80	3		23	1
	-81	2		20	1
	-83	1		19	1
	-85	1		25	1
	-87	1		27	1
	-89	1		23	1
	-93	3		30	4
	-96	1		31	1
	-95	1		33	1
	-98	2		32	1
	-99	1		31	2
	-87	1		34	1
	-102	1		35	4
	Total:	**28**		**Total:**	**28**

Data in Tables 8.13 and 8.14 strongly suggest that significant differences existed in the social skills development as reported by teachers and parents. Significant percent differences were reported by both teachers and parents. Teachers tended to rate social behavior growth higher. Results supported the hypothesis stating that parents and teachers would perceive the social skills development of African-American males as positive after they had participated in a structured social skills program.

Significant differences reported in Tables 8.13 and 8.14 strongly supported the major hypothesis of this study. That there will be a significant differences in the reading and mathematics achievement of African-American males after they have participated in a year-long structured program in social skills development. All measures were significant beyond the .01 level of confidence.

Discussion

Generally, most of the African-American males in this study were pleased with their progress and voiced an interest in continuing with the program. Both teachers and parents were also pleased with the significant social and academic gains that students had made.

This study, based on the findings of this investigation, implies that there is a vital need to intervene and teach social skills to young African-American males at an early age. Data from this study tended to support the premise that deficits in social skills development can be compensated for young African-American males if early systematic planning is conducted between the home and school.

In analyzing the statistical data as to the project's effectiveness, there is a need to proceed cautiously, however. Deficiencies in the research design involved a failure to determine actual achievement in reading and mathematics, attitudes toward school, length of time of the project in the school. In addition, involvement of the school in other experimental programs may have added to and impacted the positive results. Nevertheless, the project appeared to have significantly changed the negative and aggressive behaviors of the boys, expanded self-images, and increased achievement in reading and mathematics. Improvement is needed if the program is to be strengthened; thus, the following recommendations are made:

1. The total resources of the school should be used and integrated in order to bring about desired changes in behavior.

2. Additional studies should be attempted in other schools to see if the results of this study can be replicated.

3. Parents must become an integral part of all planning designed to improve social skills of their children.

4. Studies should be designed to follow up on the progress of the project and study the boys over a span of three or four years to determine the long-term effect of the structured social skills program on behavior.

Summary

Three experimental studies were conducted to determine the impact of a structured social skills program on academic and interpersonal skills, attendance, and office referrals of African-American males in grade 1 and 2. All of the boys participated in a year-long structured social skills training program. All measures showed significant growth between pre-

and post-testing. These studies add to the increasing body of knowledge related to the value of systematically teaching social skills to young African-American males. Data suggest that deficits in social skills development can be compensated for if intervention is attempted early. It is recommended that a drug component be added to future research of this nature.

Chapter 9

Social/International Skills Curriculum for Young African-American Males

Curriculum Development: An Overview

Curriculum development is designed to reflect the course of study in schools. It is intended to present information to students in an organized manner through various instructional methods and strategies. Teachers must be cognizant of creative and innovative ways to individualize and maximize learning for pupils by providing practical learning activities (Beane 1990, Kristo, 1982; Ross, 1993; Gruenewald, 1990).

According to Beane, et al (Beane, 1993; Dodge, 1988; Hedley, 1990), designing curriculum involves two major methodologies. The first methodology is experimental instruction. Experimental instruction is designed to intrinsically motivate students interests inside and outside of the classroom. The second approach, systematic instruction, involves teacher/student interaction. The major purpose of systematic instruction is to develop a skill of concept and design materials and activities that enable students to achieve the selected objectives.

Curriculum development in most school districts is concerned with developing academics in order to equip pupils to master the complex tasks presented by our society. This approach is valid for most pupils. However, due to poor social and interpersonal skills development of many minority and young African-American males, social skill development may be necessary before academic skills can be mastered.

It is generally agreed by most professionals in the field of education that schools should be involved in teaching social and interpersonal skills. For example, social skills education and interpersonal skills development are ideal ways to reach responsibility for self and others and for exploring the meaning of human interaction and relationships. The subject is too important and complex for the home to handle alone.

A social skills curriculum can also help students understand: (1) how to develop self-esteem along with their emotions and how their emotions affects others; (2) how to develop positive social relationships; (3) respect for others; (4) respect for rules and regulations; (5) ways to develop moral and character; (6) ways to examine one's values; (7) ways to make responsible choices; (8) their potential and worth as human beings; (9) how to develop a sense of responsibility toward others and ways of behaving appropriately in public places; (10) the role and duty of responsible citizens; and (11) how to develop effective communication skills; (12) know that medicine taken in abundance may be harmful; (13) know the difference between taking medicine from someone trusted vs someone not known; (14) know that drugs can affect behavior and how one thinks, (15) recognize dangers in taking drugs; (16) know how to be assertive and how to resist peer pressure; and (17) know the relationship between drug abuse, HIV, AIDS, and STDS.

Curriculum strategies-outlined in this text are designed to address the social skills and others as they relate specifically to young African-American school-age males. Experimental, direct and systematic curriculum methodologies will be employed, which is designed to intergrade developing social skills with the after mentioned steps.

The phenomenon of educating African-American school-aged males has been studied an investigated extensively, resulting in numerous educators advocating that these "special" young males demonstrate inappropriate social skills/behaviors inside as well as outside the classroom. Developing the appropriate social skills for successful interaction with peers and significant adults (teachers, parents) can be considered one of the most important accomplishments of childhood and early adolescence should be addressed as soon as possible. This is particularly true in the area of establishing and maintaining relations with peers and authority figures. Not only can social skills deficits have a negative impact on future interpersonal functioning, it may also affect current functioning, reducing the quality and quantity of the learning experiences to which students are exposed in their educational settings (Furnham, 1986).

Developing the appropriate social skills for successful interaction with peers and significant adults (teachers, parents) can be considered one of the most important accomplishments of childhood and early adolescence should be addressed as soon as possible. This is particularly true in the area of establishing and maintaining relations with peers and authority figures. Not only can social skills deficits have a negative impact on future interpersonal functioning, it may also affect current functioning, reducing the quality and quantity of the learning experiences to which students are exposed in their educational settings (Furnham, 1986).

Social skills have been defined as goals-oriented, rule-governed, situation-specific learned behaviors that vary according to social context. Social skills involving both observable and non-observable cognitive and affective elements that help elicit positive or neutral responses and avoid negative responses from other (Brody, 1977; Collins, 1992; DiMartino, 1990; Dorr-Bremme, 1992; Furnham, 1986). As such, social behavior constitutes an intricate interfactional process. As a result, the behavior of school-aged children is influenced by that of their partners (e.g., teachers, mentors, tutors, and peers). These interactions should prepare young African-American males to deal effectively with physical and emotional problems, in society, including drugs and alcohol.

Society expects that when children reach various developmental stages, they will demonstrate greater foresight and more controlled behaviors. Society also expects that children will be capable, not only of meeting increased demands within learning tasks, but also more complex, subtle social situations. Failure to meet these expectations may increase their sense of social alienation and helplessness.

The curriculum presented here is designed to enable young African-American males to become socially contributing members of society by meeting expected standards. Strategies have been developed to assist educators in providing these students appropriate social skills training to enable them to operate successfully in the schools and society. Intervention techniques have been selected based upon research techniques to assist young Black males in controlling aggression, assuming responsibility, becoming productive members of the group, and to say "No" to drugs.

The author highly endorses that proactive approach be employed when teaching social skills to young African-American males. Since proactive instruction provides children with social intervention before negative behaviors occur, this approach is preferable to reactive teaching. Whereas proactive instruction teaches social skills before social rejection is experienced, reactive instruction waits for the individual to fail and then applies intervention strategies. Many young African-American males have problems developing appropriate social skills due to the problems outlined throughout the text. Proactive instruction will prevent many of the negative consequences of inappropriate social skills, as well as improve the self-image of young African-American males.. Recommended strategies for proactive instruction may assist the boys in:
1. dealing positively with accusations
2. accepting the feelings of others in a non threatening manner
3. respecting the feelings of others
4. avoiding fights and conflicts
5. dealing effectively with teasing
6. giving praise or compliments to others
7. accepting compliments from others
8. apologizing for inappropriate behavior
9. expressing anger in a positive way
10. showing affection and appreciation toward others
11. practicing self-control
12. knowing about the harmful effects on taking drugs
13. knowing how to be assertive.
These instructional activities may be expanded or modified as needed.

As indicated throughout this book, young African-American males must be taught appropriate social skills if they are going to be contributing members of society. The social skills outlined here should be infused throughout the curriculum and integrated as needed by the teacher. These strategies are seen as immediate, useful resources for teaching pro-social skills to young African-American males. It is a how-to-do guide, providing specific examples and strategies for teachers and other professionals. Additionally, the curriculum is based upon indepth research and years of teaching and observing the social skills of young African-American males.

A Functional Approach

A functional approach to teaching social skills to young African-American males can easily be infused throughout the curriculum. A functional approach involves exposing the learner to real-life situations, concepts, and activities such as self-identity, acquiring self-concept, achieving social acceptable behavior, bonding respecting the rights of others, maintaining good interpersonal skills, achieving independence, employing problem-solving skills, taking turns, and communicating appropriately with others.

Several group activities, such as role playing, modeling, individual groups, dramatic play, reviewing plans and video tapes, and cooperative groups may be used to teach social skills to young African-American males from a functional and holistic viewpoint within the context of real-life experiences. In essence, children are taught to model, imitate, and demonstrate appropriate social skills in the reality in which they exist (McGinnis & Goldstein, 1984).

Curriculum Development

A social skills curriculum should be based upon those social skills needed to function successfully in one's society. Much of the research reviewed indicated that a significant number of young African-American males have not mastered the social skills needed to function successfully in our society (Gibbs, 1991; Holland, 1993; Obia kor, 1990; Taylor, 1993; Hilliard, 1988).

The initial step in developing a social skills curriculum is to identify those general social behaviors that are critical to successful social functioning. These general social behaviors are then rewritten as general objectives, which provide the framework for constructing other components of the curriculum.

The second stage is to sequence specific objectives as they relate to the general objectives. All specific objectives are designed to achieve the general objectives... Specific objectives are stated in behavioral and measurable terms. The third step is to identify activities and resources that can achieve the stated objectives. (Refer to Appendix F for selected resources). Activities should be functional and reflect real-life experiences that young African-American males are exposed to As much as possible, parents should be involved in reinforcing the social skills taught. Parents may be used as resource individuals and may offer suggestions relative to material and activities. (See chapter 7 for specific strategies for involving parents.)

The fourth step is to include cultural, ethnic, and racial diversity into the curriculum. This approach affords young African-American males the opportunity to appreciate and understand their own self-worth and sense of importance and belonging as well as identify Blacks and other minorities who have made significant contribution in several fields. An additional benefit is that the young Black males can identify and associate with appropriate role models.

A curriculum that does not highlight the contributions of Blacks and minorities gives an inaccurate and distorted view of the many significant contributions made by the. Multicultural activities and strategies enriches the curriculum by showing differences in cultural styles, patterns, and interests of diverse groups. The social skills unit should be related with the developmental and grade levels of the young African-American ales.

Assessment of Social Skills

Assessment is long-term and continuous. This process is designed to monitor how effectively a strategy is achieving a desired goal. Both self-monitoring by students and teacher monitoring are recommended . Most students welcome the opportunity to be involved in monitoring their own progress toward attaining a skill. Chapter 4 overviews selected social assessment techniques.

Social Skills Unit

General Objective No. 1 of the Unit:

Young African-American males will achieve socially acceptable behaviors in social and interpersonal situations.

Specific Objectives:

    A.. The boys will respect members of the opposite sex.

    B. The boys will demonstrate appropriate character traits needed for acceptance in the public.

    C. The boys will demonstrate proper behavior in public places.

    D. The boys will show respect for the rights and properties of others.

    E. The boys will recognize authority and follow instructions of school, home, and the community.

F.   The boys will recognize personal roles in public places.

G.   The boys will use terms such as "please," "thank you," and "excuse me" at the appropriate times and places.

H.   The boys will practice sportsmanship by sharing toys and information.

I.   The boys will stand in line without bothering others.

J.   Given a description of behavior on the bus, the boys will show appropriate behavior.

K.   The boys will know how and when to give and accept apologies.

L.   The boys will know when to be asserted and resist peer pressure when offered drugs.

Recommended Activities: (individualize and expand as needed)

A..   The boys will respect members of the opposite sex.

1.   Role play a variety of situations showing the boys how to show respect for females.

2.   During everyday activities and conversations, require the boys to say "please," "thank you," and "excuse me" to the girls.

3.   If the boys curse at or call the girls derogatory names, try to distract them. Intervene by defining the word or words, and indicate that these are words that hurt people.

4.   Show the boys pictures of children working and playing together; point out that both boys and girls are playing and working together and that both sexes are respecting each other.

5.   Reward the boys when they show appropriate behavior toward girls.

6.   Assign girls and boys to group activities. Assign equal responsibilities to girls.

B.   The boys will demonstrate appropriate character traits and behaviors needed for acceptance in the public.

1.   Provide activities that the boys required to assist in structured activities.

2.   Demonstrate to the boys how to move in crowds by saying "excuse me," "pardon me," when people are blocking the way.

3.   Model appropriate behavior when meeting new people and in all activities where the boys come in contact with the public.

4.   Explain and demonstrate to students how to observe safety rules and how to be very considerate of others when using public transportation.

5.   Role play a variety of situations that might occur when the boys are using public transportation. Demonstrate socially acceptable behaviors in these situations.

6.   Demonstrate, show films, and model appropriate behaviors for the boys to demonstrate when receiving services from the barber shop, banks,, stores, or any other public places.

7.   Role play a variety of situations where the boys demonstrate appropriate behavior when receiving public service.

8.   Show the boys how to greet people in a socially acceptable language in public.

C. Repeat steps 1 through 8 in Section B.

D. The boys will show respect for the rights and properties of others.

1.   Provide activities where the boys are required to cooperate with other properties.

2.   Role play activities where the boys are required to cooperate with others for the success and welfare of the group.

3.   Initiate a variety of games and activities that require the boys to share or take turns.

4.   Provide activities for the boys to share games and discuss the importance of protecting others' properties.

5.   Allow time for the boys to bring their games to school to share with the class. Emphasize the importance of safeguarding personal property.

6.   Discuss vandalism. Draw from the experiences of the boys. Discuss the legal aspects of vandalism in terms that the boys can understand.

7. Provide activities where the boys verbally
   compliment their classmates.
E. The boys will recognized authority and follow
    instructions at school, home, and the community.
    1. Through films, videotapes, and
        demonstrations, show the boys how to
        respond appropriately to authority and
        establish rules, supervised and unsupervised.
        Have the boys narrate or draw appropriate
        ways of responding to authority.
    2. Provide time for boys to share with the class
        appropriate ways of responding to authorities.
    3. Discuss the importance of rules and laws.
        Summarize the importance of classroom rules.
        What purpose do they serve and why it is
        important to obey them?
        4. Plan an activity where a rule is broken. Have
           the boys discuss the consequences of
           breaking the rule. Discuss how it affects
           others. List the consequences of the
           behavior.
    5. When the boys break a rule, explain the
        consequences and demonstrate alternate
        ways of solving or addressing the problem.
        6. Invitee a law enforcement officer to speak to
            the boys. Encourage interaction between the
            boys and the officer.
        7. Encourage parents to establish rules at home
            for the boys and follow and discuss the
            consequences of breaking rules.
        8. Role play and show films where individuals
            break laws and are held responsible for their
            actions. Discuss alternative ways of
            responding to the situations.
F. The boys will recognize personal roles in pubic places.
    1. Read the boys stories of high interest in which the
        characters accept responsibilities for their
        behaviors.

2.   Role play a variety of conditions in which the boys are required to make decisions; both appropriate and inappropriate.

3.   When a situation arises where the boys have broken a rule, discuss the consequences of such behavior. When possible, involve the boys in selecting the consequences.

4.   Develop activities stressing that when one acts inappropriately, one must accept the consequences of the behavior.

5.   Encourage the boys to think about the outcomes of their behaviors by providing situations in which they must make choices.

G.   The boys will use terms such as "please," "thank you," and "excuse me," at appropriate times.

1.   During everyday activities, infuse conversations where the boys will use terms such as "excuse me," "thank you," etc., at appropriate times. Reward the boys for positive responses.

2.   Role play a variety of situations requiring courteous responses from the boys.

3.   Encourage the boys to use good manners as consumers, through demonstrations and dramatic everyday activities.

4.   Provide activities where the boys are required to model behaviors. Praise successful attempts and discuss why others are not successful.

5.   Demonstrate to the boys how to move throw crowds by saying "excuse me," "may I please pass?," etc.

H.   The boys will practice sportmanship by sharing toys and information.

1.   As the boys play and work together, provide activities where they must take turns and share materials. Praise the boys when their attempts are successful.

2.   Discuss the concept of "a good sport." Encourage the boys to accept success and

failure in sports and games. Praise the boys for being a "good sport," a "good loser" as well as a "good winner."

3. In the school, infuse activities within the curriculum that require that the boys take turns, such as dramatic play activities that can only be successfully completed through teamwork and cooperation.

4. When the boys lose, encourage them to try again. Discuss the idea that losing is a part of winning. Provide activities that allow the boys to win sometimes.

I. The boys will stand in line without bothering others.

1. Model and demonstrate appropriate behavior while in line. Praise and reward the boys for appropriate behavior.

2. Role play situations where the boys show appropriate behavior in line.

3. Discuss the importance of following rules. Relate how appropriately standing in line is obeying rules.

4. Demonstrate to the boys how standing in line without bothering others is respecting the rights of others.

5. Relate showing appropriate behavior in line to "good citizenship."

J. Given a description of behavior on the bus, the boys will show appropriate behavior.

1. Provide appropriate models for the boys to follow when riding on buses.

2. Demonstrate how to handle situations such as pushing, stepping on toes, loud language, etc., while riding on buses.

3. Role play a variety of situations appropriate and inappropriate, while riding on the bus.

4. Review films and filmstrips showing appropriate and inappropriate behaviors and have the boys evaluate both types of situations and provide alternative solutions.

K.   The boys will know how and when to use rational processes to check their emotions.
  1. After a fight or disturbance, from a circle and play a game before discussing the incident.
  2. Sing a favorite song with the boys before trying to settle an issue.

L.   The boys will know when to be asserted and resist peer pressure when offered drugs.
  1. Review how to make appropriate choices.
  2. Teach the effects of mind altering drugs.
  3. Model and demonstrate how drugs can lead to self destruction.
  4. Teach the boys how to be assertive and to resist peer-pressure.
  5. Show and discuss pictures.
  6. Draw from the boys experiences.

General Objectives No.2 of the Unit:

Young African-American males will show positive self-concepts when dealing with others.

Specific Objectives:

A. They boys will know how and when to use rational processes to evaluate their emotions.

B. The boys will emphasize their special uniqueness by recognizing their potential.

C. The boys will recognize the impact of their behavior on others.

D. The boys will personally and positively interact with each other.

E. The boys will show how they can reduce negative repercussions in the classroom.

F. Have the boys to demonstrate special traits of each other.

G. The boys will demonstrate and model behaviors that will enhance their self-image and concepts.

H. Have the boys demonstrate and discuss ways that they can effectively deal with their fears.

I. The boys will learn to say "NO" to drugs.

Recommended Activities: (individualized and expand as needed)

A.   The boys will know how and when to use rational processed to evaluate their emotions.

    1.   Have the boys choose an attitude they would like to make into an attitude mask: angry, happy, sad, tired, bored, scared, sick; encourage a large variety of feelings. Provide materials for the boys to make the masks. While they are making the masks, ask them to be thinking about how their masks will "act" after completion; have them share with each other.

    2.   Choose both positive and negative feelings masks to role play each situation.

    3.   Have the boys identify the major emotions felt most of the time: happy, sad, and angry, scared, and tired. Have them associate a color with each of the emotions. Use mobiles when identifying the boys' emotions.

    4.   Have the boys to identify people being angry from pictures. Discuss the following:

        a.   Why is this person angry?

        b.   Have you ever been angry?

        c.   What makes you really, really, really, angry?

        d.   What do you do when you get angry?

    5.   Discuss some ways to handle anger. Categorize and list on chart paper. Praise the boys for controlling anger in the classroom.

    6.   Assign boys the tasks of interviewing a significant other about a problem he had and how it was solved. Films that focus on a central character with a   problem t o solve serve as good models for the boys and are catalysts for class discussion. The boys should first discuss their problems in small groups. Teammates can then contribute ideas for resolution as well as just being supportive.

    7.   Teach the following problem-solving steps to the boys:

        a.   What is the problem?

    b.   Think of solutions.

    c.   Select the two or three preferred solutions.

    d.   What might happen if they were chosen?

    e.   Choose the best solution after reviewing the consequences.

    f.   Make a plan.

    g.   Do it!

8.   Write down messages that can be disruptive to a class environment. This exercise assists the boys in recognizing how deadly put-down are to other's feelings. It also helps them find ways to change negative responses to more positive ones.

9.   Divide the boys into teams. Have the boys make a set of 10 index cards for each team. Instruct them to write a different negative statement on each card. Each team selects one boy to be the dealer who passes out the cards. Each team member reads one put-down message to the group. After each reading the team gives messages that could be said instead. The team gives   messages that could be said instead. The team chooses the best answer to each put-down statement and records them on chart paper.

10.   Provide activities for group discussion by showing a picture of emotions taking control. Have the boys give alternative ways to solve the problem.

B.   The boys will emphasize their special uniqueness by recognizing their potential.

1.   Tell the boys that they are going to be learning about a very special person. Who is the most special person in the whole world? When a boy comes up with the answer that he is the most special person in the world, praise the boy.

2.   Show the boys a stuffed animal with a price tag. "How much are YOU worth?" Discuss with the boys that they are PRICELESS. You are worth more than all the stuffed animals in the world.

3.	A circle is formed and an objective in passed around. Each boy is instructed to say something positive about the boy passing the object to him.

4.	Have the boys draw pictures about things that they can do successfully. Emphasize the point tat all of us have the potential for being successful.

5.	Instruct the boys to keep records of their achievements. As they accomplish each of their achievements they have written down and drawn. The teacher periodically inspects and evaluates the record, making appropriate positive remarks.

6.	Encourage the boys to think about things they like about themselves and things they wish they could change. Remind them that there are some things we can change and other things that we cannot change. Discuss with the boys things they can and cannot change.

7.	Construct mobiles that have silhouettes of the boys as the center. From the Silhouettes, hang words, magazine "specialties" of the boys. The boys' name will appear in big letters on the silhouettes.

C.	The boys will recognize the impact of their behaviors on others.

1.	Use a hand puppet to demonstrate how negative behaviors, such as saying unkind words to others, can have a negative impact on them.

2.	Discuss with the boys how they can choose to treat others in a positive way. Pictures or puppets may be used.

3.	Group the boys in a circle and have them relate how other people's behaviors have had a negative impact upon them. Solicit solutions from the boys as to how these behaviors can be changed to positive ones.

4.	Use creative dramatics and role playing showing how the negative impact of behaviors displayed by others can have an impact on them.

5.	Provide activities and examples to assist the boys in internalizing their behaviors, such as thinking out loud before acting and examining the consequences of their behaviors on others.

6.   Role play activities showing fair and unfair treatment of others. Outline how unfair treatment may become fair.

D.   Provide activities for the boys to interact positively with each other.

1.   For each hour of the clock, have the boys fill in a different classmate's name. Encourage them to initiate the meeting with the classmate by introducing themselves. Model to the boys how to make appropriate introductions.

2.   Write each boy's name on a slip of paper and put all slips into a small container. As the container is passed, each boy draws the name of another boy and says what is special about him. No negative comments are allowed. This activity requires a great deal of time to complete.

3.   Choose a boy to be the recipient of the greeting for the day. Each boy writes a compliment to the chosen person. At the end of the day, the recipient collects all the messages from the class.

4.   Encourage the boys to write messages to a peer on special occasions.

5.   Have each boy find a special character in a magazine. Give the character a name, place, and date of birth, family friends, and occupation. Have the boys describe how his special person feels.

E.   Demonstrate ways that the boys can reduce negative repercussions in the classroom.

1.   Provide scenarios for the boys to discuss and role play negative behaviors such as:

a. Suppose that by telling your friend you are angry with him, he becomes angry with you? Stress the fact that frequently holding feelings inside may avoid conflicts.

b. If someone called you ugly or stupid, how would you react?
How would you control your feelings?

c. Suppose someone said, "I have you: get out of my way!"

        d. Suppose someone said, "I don't like you."

        e. Suppose someone calls you stupid.

2. Provide opportunities for the boys to be involved in constructing classroom rules as well as the consequences for violating the rules.

3. Demonstrate to the boys that all of us at times have many feelings; some that we can control and others that get out of control. Today we are going to discuss ways we can reduce negative feelings inside of us.

4. Use a hand puppet. Make the puppet look shy, scared, happy, and sad. The puppet should elicit empathy from the boys as they identify with some of the puppet's feelings. Have the boys discuss how they would handle their feelings.

F. Provide activities showing special traits of the boys.

1. Give each boy a piece of paper; the pieces of paper are divided into squares. Have them draw and past pictures, photographs, and souvenirs about who he is. When all squares are completed, they can be taped together and displayed as a scrapbook.

2. Instruct the boys to complete a promotional piece (poem, story, picture, etc.) about themselves.

3. Have promotional information shared with the class in order that they can affirm themselves in front of others.

4. Provide opportunities for the boys to share information about themselves. Use the shared information to determine things that the boys have in common. Have the information shared with the class. This activity may assist in developing the self-concept of shy boys.

5. Videotape the boys performing positive behaviors. Show the tape to the class and accent the positive behaviors.

6. Develop a Citizen of the Week Award. Give certificates to the boys who meet the established criteria.

G. Demonstrate, plan, and model behaviors that enhance the self-images and concepts of the boys.

1. Help students develop an accurate self-description by modeling acceptable behaviors.
2. Model behaviors showing the boys how not to be oversensitive to criticism.
3. Plan activities that assist the boys in clarifying or thinking more about themselves, such as showing photographs and telling stories about themselves.
4. Give examples of how the boys can make positive statements about self and others.
5. Provide opportunities for the boys to discover major sources of influence upon self.
6. Make tokens to give out to the boys who have been "caught doing something good."
7. Construct a mobile and hang from it words and phrases that are used in your classroom to promote positive behaviors such as:

    "Thank You"   "Excuse Me"
    "Good Morning" "I Like You"
    "I Forgive You" "May I Help?"
    "I'm Sorry"   "Can I Help?

H. Demonstrate and discuss ways that the boys can effectively deal with their fears.

1. Structure group activities where the boys can discuss their fears. Emphasize the fact that all of us have fears at one time or another.
2. Using chart paper, make a list of some of the fears stated by the boys. Discuss ways of minimizing fears.
3. Have the boys use pictures to discuss the types of fears shown and what can be done to reduce the levels of fear.
4. Develop dramatic activities showing how fear may be reduced in the following areas:
    a. Someone making fun of you
    b. Being left out of an important activity or event.
    c. Parents divorcing.
    d. Presenting before a group or the class.
    e. Afraid of making a mistake.
    f. Moving to another community.

5.   Write and develop stories about fears, indicating a solution for controlling them.

6.   Have the boys share some of their past fears with the class and explain how they overcame them.

I.   The boys will learn to say "No" to drugs.

    1.   Show videotapes and films concerning the misuse and abuse of drugs.

    2.   Model how to say "No" to drugs.

    3.   Have boys to relate some of their experiences.

    4.   Develop a list of phrases for refusing drugs.

    5.   Have boys to develop stories and share with the class.

    6.   Make pictures and discuss with the class.

General Objective No. 3 of the Unit:

Young African-American males will identify and evaluate their feelings about others.

Specific Objectives:

A.   The boys will realize that other people have feelings and understanding what can be done to help them feel better about themselves.

B.   The boys will be made aware of how their anger can affect the feelings and well-being of others.

C.   The boys will demonstrate activities showing the impact of negative behaviors on self and others.

D.   Have the boys demonstrate the value of accepting praise

E.   The boys will show how to effectively identify and appropriately express their emotions and attitudes.

F.   Have the boys emphasize that it is important to discuss their fears with someone who can assist them.

G   Have the boys to assess and evaluate the various types of feelings shown in pictures and films.

H.   The boys will show feelings of sympathy and goodwill toward others.

I.   The boys will know not to take medicine from someone they don't know or trust.

Recommended Activities: (individualize and expanded as needed)

A.   Assist the boys in realizing that other people have feelings and what can be done to help people feel better about themselves.

    1.   Show pictures of a person feeling sad and/or scared.

Why is this person sad? What do you think happened to her/him? What could he/she do to change those scary, sad feelings?

Through pictures, show and emphasize that not everyone is afraid of the same things. Individuals express different feelings toward different things.

2. Discuss with the boys the fact that we have all experienced times when we have so many feelings inside us at the same time that we feel like we cannot handle them. We can control some of our feelings.

3. Instruct the boys that the use of negative phrases and words such as "shut up," "you're stupid," "go away," "get out of her," and "leave me alone" do not make people feel good about themselves.

4. Use puppets to show different feelings. Pose the following questions to the boys:

   a. How did the puppet choose to act out his feelings the first time?

   b. How did he act the second time? Why? Just like we choose our eating habits, we also choose our feelings. We can choose to feel good about ourselves, or we can choose to feel bad about ourselves. We can choose to treat people in positive ways when we express our feelings, or we can choose to handle situations in a negative manner and keep all our feelings inside. Which is easier: letting our feelings out in a positive way or keeping them in? Which is healthier?

B. Make the boys aware of how their anger can affect the feelings and well-being of others.

1. Discuss incidents of angry behaviors in groups, highlighting how the angry behaviors affected others in the group.

2. Show pictures of angry expressions. Discuss how other means of expressing anger could be used.

3. Using pictures, films, stories, etc., have the boys discuss what might have caused the anger. How could the incident have been prevented?

4. Teach the boys techniques that enable them to control their anger, such as being sensitive to feedback and evaluating their behaviors.
5. Instruct the boys on how anger is manifested. Highlight the physical and social aspects.
6. Using role playing and creative dramatics to demonstrate various stages of anger. Discuss alternate ways of expressing anger.
7. Develop short stories and plays showing how anger can be expressed in a positive fashion.
8. Model various stages of anger for the boys along with techniques for controlling it.

C. Provide activities showing the impact of negative behaviors on self and others.
1. Discuss with the boys how negative behaviors impact others.
2. Through the use of pictures, discuss how negative behaviors are influencing the characters in the pictures.
3. Have the boys role play negative behaviors, reflecting their impact on others.
4. Develop short skits with the boys portraying how negative behaviors influence others.
5. Using a variety of media, art, painting, etc., have the boys develop stories displaying the consequences of negative behaviors on oneself and others.
6. Use puppets to show the negative impact of behaviors on others. Ask the boys how they feel about themselves when they are happy? sad? mad? Use the puppets to demonstrate the behaviors boys would like to show.
7. Say something unkind to the puppet; have it sit up tall and shape his/her head "no" as if to refuse to accept the negative remark.

D. Demonstrate to the boys the value of accepting praise.
1. Role play incidents showing the boys how not to be uncomfortable with praise.
2. Discuss with the boys how not to become embarrassed when accepting praise.

3.   Review films and videotapes showing males accepting praise.
4.   Model appropriate behaviors for accepting praise.
5.   Have the boys share their experiences in accepting praise.
6.   Model appropriate behavior showing the boys how to apologize.
7.   Praise the boys when they have accomplished a positive task or displayed positive behaviors.

E.   Develop strategies for effectively identifying and appropriately expressing emotions and attitudes.
1.   Discuss with the boys how what they feel affects the way the behave. Use the puppets to help illustrate. Have the boys identify the puppets' feelings by demonstrating various moods. Ask the boys to demonstrate when they are glad, angry, or sad.
2.   Make a booklet for each boy. Make a special key for each booklet so the boys can readily recognize their booklet. Review the keys frequently with the boys until they can remember them. Have the boys write the secret feeling or feelings that are very special to them inside their booklets and lock them up to keep them safe.
3.   Have the boys look through magazines. Fine pictures of people who have great smiles. Cut out the smiles and paste them on the cover of books. Now look at the cover. How does it make you feel?
4.   Ask the boys to articulate their feelings and listen to the feelings of others during story and sharing time.
5.   Create scenarios expressing emotions and attitudes. Scenarios should be both negative and positive. Have the boys group and classify the scenarios based on how they would act.
6.   Using the information from #5, have the boys draw pictures. Discuss and critique each picture.

F.   Emphasize to the boys that it is important to discuss their fears with someone who can assist them.
1.   List and categorize fears with boys. Stress the fact that fears are often a result of our perceptions of a situation, rather than the danger being inherent in

the situation. Instruct the boys to discuss their fears with parents, pastor, counselor, relatives, close friends. Ask them to seek their opinions and advice.

2. Ask the boys to discus their fears. Encourage them to explain and identify what the fears are. Provide suggestions for dealing with the fears.

3. Relate to the boys that most fears are imaginary. Have the boys write their fears on a piece of paper and place them in a paper bag. Pull fears from the bag and separate real fears from imaginary fears. Discuss both types of fears.

4. Use puppets to demonstrate various stages of imaginary fears.

5. From the list of fears in #1, discuss with the boys how these fears may be minimized or corrected.

6. Role play how fears originate and how many of them are based upon uncertainties, doubts, rumors, and untruths.

7. Discuss with the boys and demonstrate how many fears are needed and useful.

G. Show pictures, films, and videotapes and model behaviors about individuals expressing feelings. Provide opportunities for the boys to assess and evaluate the various types of feelings.

1. Collect magazine pictures of people's faces expressing different feelings: surprise, contentment, anxiety, anger, grief, etc. Have the boys study the picture and decide the circumstances that led to the emotion shown. This technique may be used individually or in groups.

2. Emphasize the importance of feelings by stressing that feelings make our lives rich and exciting, but that they can cause us problems depending upon how we act on those feelings as well as how we deal with them.

3. Instruct the boys to reflect about things they feel good about in others and compare to their own feelings.

4. Develop cooperative groups. Have the boys role play certain feelings such as sad, happy, upset,

disagreeing, and agreeing. Have other groups critique the feelings and give alternative ways they could have dealt with their feelings.

5. Review films and videotapes where people express different feelings. Have the boys group and classify them.

6. Write stories expressing different feelings. Have the boys share with the class.

7. Instruct the boys that it is okay to show feelings, sympathy, and respect toward others.

8. Use puppets to demonstrate and show feeling and respect toward others.

H. The boys will know not to take medicine from someone they do not know or trust.

9. Teach the boys that every day items such as coffee, vitamins, and plants may be harmful.

10. Instruct the boys not to take drugs or medicines without adult supervision.

11. Role play how peer pressure is used to promote drug usage.

12. Use puppets to demonstrate how to refuse taking medicine.

General Objective No. 4 of the Unit:

Young African-American males will use appropriate communication skills to develop new friendships and rekindle old ones.

Specific Objectives:

A. Review the importance of communication skills in developing appropriate interpersonal skills.

B. Develop activities and games to better acquaint the boys with each other.

C. Discuss the meaning of friendship. Outline ways that friendships may be developed.

D. Identify and articulate the characteristics of a good friend.

E. Provide the boys with the knowledge to distinguish between friendly and unfriendly actions.

F. Provide activities for the boys to address the group on several points of interest. Develop criteria to evaluate the topics.

G.   Invite other classes to group activities such as talks and games; elicit their input.

H.   The boy will understand that taking medicines in abundance may be harmful.

Recommended Activities: (individualize and expand as needed)

A.   Review the importance of communication skills in developing appropriate interpersonal skills. Communication is an important component in developing social skills. The following are suggestions for building a communicative environment for the classroom. When used at the beginning, these exercises can help the boys rekindle old friendships and develop new ones.

1.   Review with the boys the relationship between communication skills and developing appropriate interpersonal skills.

2.   Teach the boys how to properly express themselves in public places.

3.   Provide activities to make the boys aware of appropriate language to use at public and social function.

4.   Model techniques for teaching the boys how to monitor their oral expression at social functions.

5.   Have the boys critique each others' communication skills while demonstrating social and interpersonal skills.

6.   Use high-profile individuals to compare their communication and interpersonal skills with those of the boys.

7.   Provide many activities for the boys to express themselves.

B.   Develop activities and games to better acquaint the boys with each other.

1.   Instruct the boys how to play "people hunt." Have the boys move around the classroom in order to learn more about their classmates. Tell the boys to more abut for five minutes to collect a different classmate's signature for

each item on the list. The list could contain
items such as the following:

a.   has a bird for a pet
b.   has black hair
c.   has the shortest hair in the room
d.   like popcorn
e.   has two brother
f.   has one sister
g.   is the oldest child in the family
h.   has been on a fishing trip
i.   likes science best of all school
      subjects
j.   was born in June
k.   has won a medal in a sports
      competition

2.   Group the boys by special characteristics
      such as birthdays. Have the boys indicate
      what day of the month they were born.
3.   Provide activities for the boys to share their
      interests with the class. Classmates with
      similar interests may be invited to share
      their experiences.
4.   Have the boys write stories about their
      favorite friends. Have the boys identify
      similar characteristics between them.

C.   Discuss the meaning of friendship. Outline ways
      that friendships may be developed.
1.   Divide students into terms of three or four
      and provide each boy with a form. Inform
      the boys that, as a team, they must decide
      on a list of characteristics they all agree are
      important in a friend. Have them list three
      characteristics on the form.
2.   Each team must work together to rank the
      characteristics on order of importance.
      Review with the boys that the characteristic
      they have agreed upon is the most
      important should be listed as number 1,
      number 2, and so on. Instruct the boys to
      complete the remainder of the form by

themselves. Tell the boys to look over the form and decide which characteristics can best be applied to themselves.

3. Explain to the boys that sometimes when working in a group, positions or ideas have to be agreed upon so that the group can come to a decision. Have the boys share their experiences with the group process and determine whether they can come up with a group answer. If the boys have different answers, ask them to describe their answers to the large group.

4. Have the boys share their forms with the class.

5. Discuss with the boys what constitutes good friendship. What are the components of good friendship?

6. Summarize how friendships may be developed and maintained.

7. Develop the concept that it is "okay" for boys to develop friendships with girls.

D. Identify and articulate the characteristics of a good friend.

1. Discuss the characteristics of a good friend. Ask the boys to list at least five important friendship attributes, such as humor, availability, kindness, loyalty, and common interests.

2. Write characteristics that are suggested on the chalkboard. Refer to them again and add to them as the class thinks of new descriptions. Encourage the boys to write their own "recipes" for how to make a friend

3. Have the boys work in teams to develop a mutually agreed-upon recipe. The team's final recipe can be written on an index card in a "recipe" format. A cookbook may be used as a guide.

4.   Instruct the boys to draw pictures relevant to characteristics or attributes of good friendship.

5.   Using pictures and photographs, have the boys identify attributes of a good friendship.

6.   Have the boys write stories about how they met their best friends.

E.   Provide the boys with the knowledge of distinguish between friendly and unfriendly actions.

1.   Make a circle and cut it out. Divide the circle into at least eight parts. Cut a dial hand/spinner using a piece of plastic. Attach the spinner to the center of the wheel with a paper fastener. Ask the boys to think of ways to be friendly. Write down appropriate deeds in each section of the circle. Provide opportunity for each boy to spin the wheel and discuss the deed where the pointer stopped.

2.   Cut out and glue small photographs that the boys have brought from home onto a piece of chart paper. Have the boys classify friendly and unfriendly behaviors from the photographs.

3.   Make a chart categorizing friendly and unfriendly behaviors; record input from the boys.

4.   Identify friendly and unfriendly behaviors from stories and pictures.

5.   Assist the boys in constructing stories about friendly and unfriendly behaviors.

6.   From the list of friendly and unfriendly actions in #3, have the boys give examples of the two types of behaviors.

F.   Provide activities for the boys to address the group on several points of interests. Develop criteria for evaluating the topics.

1.   Discuss with the boys standards for evaluating reports. Include such factors as:

a.   Being polite to the speaker.

      b. Showing respect for the speaker.

      c. Not interrupting the speaker.

      d. Saving questions to the end of the presentation

      e. Giving a valid criticism for a disagreement.

  2. For boys who have similar interests, permit them to report in groups.

  3. Overview a common format for giving oral presentations. Instruct the boys that preparation is needed when giving reports.

  4. Invite the librarian to instruct the boys on library techniques and finding information on selected topics.

G. Invite other classes to group activities such as talks and games; elicit their input.

  1. Expand the circle of friends by inviting other classes to participate.

  2. Attempt to develop teams involving other boys from different classes.

  3. New teams may report to joint classes. The format for evaluating reports in #1 is used.

  4. A joint culminating activity involving all of the classes may be presented to the total school relevant to friendly and unfriendly actions.

  5. Group art projects may be developed and posted throughout the school.

H. The boys will understand that taking medicines in abundance may be harmful.

  1. Demonstrate to the boys the harmful effects of taking too much medicine

  2. Instruct the boys that overdose of any medicine may be harmful.

  3. Develop strategies for recognizing tactics promoting certain medicines.

  4. Teach the boys that most items taking in excessive amount maybe habit forming.

  5. Develop projects showing how some items may be harmful.

General Objective No. 5 of the Unit:
   Young African-American males will acquire self-confidence
and employ appropriate social skills at home, school, and the
community.

Specific Objectives:

   A.   The boys will demonstrate how to cope with their
        feelings and emotions arising from conflicts.
   B.   The boys will practice acceptable social behaviors at
        school, home, and in the community.
   C.   The boys will accept praise when given.
   D.   The boys will accept criticism when given and
        demonstrate how to use the information for self-
        improvement.
   E.   The boys will develop a sense of pride and self-
        confidence.
   F.   The boys will control their anger when provoked.
   G.   The boys will understand the impact of their
        behavior upon others
   H.   The boys will understand how drugs may affect
        social skills development.

*Recommended Activities: (individualize and expand as
needed)*

   A.   The boys will demonstrate how to cope with their
        feelings and emotions arising from conflicts.
        1. From newspapers, films, filmstrips and tapes,
            show pictures of sad, happy, and angry faces.
            Have the boys explain how the people are
            feeling.
        2. Have the boys draw faces showing a variety of
            expressions.   Have the boys discuss and
            interpret their pictures, relating how   to
            expressions can be changed.
        3. Role play conditions that may create anger
            among the boys. Model and demonstrate ways
            of controlling anger.
        4. Practice behavior intervention strategies with
            the boys to assist them in controlling anger.
            Praise the boys for successful attempts.

5. Provide activities where the boys can talk out their anger. Demonstrate how unacceptable behaviors are not appropriate ways for expressing anger. Model and demonstrate strategies.

B. The boys will practice acceptable behaviors at school, home, and in the community.

1. Discuss rules and laws with the boys. Explain that rules are made for our protection. Have the boys discuss classroom, home, and community rules.

2. When the boys break a rule, explain why obeying rules is important. Elicit responses from the boys about how rules protect us.

3. Role play situations. Show appropriate and inappropriate behaviors at school, home, and in the community. Have the boys critique each situation.

4. Show filmstrips, films, and videos of individuals displaying appropriate behavior.

5. Provide training for parents to use interpersonal skills to improve acceptable behaviors.

C. The boys will accept praise when given.

1. Develop activities such as demonstrations, role playing, modeling, and using magazines showing males accepting praise.

2. Discuss with the boys that accepting praise is not a sign of weakness, but strength; when praising, individuals are attempting to show appreciation of tasks well done.

3. Provide activities throughout the day where the boys are praised for successfully completing assigned tasks.

4. Role play activities where an authoritative male is accepting praise. Have the boys to discuss why.

D. The boys will accept criticism and use the information for self-improvement.

1. Role play situations in which the boys are ciritized by each other. Demonstrate

activities showing the boys to respond to criticisms by explaining that the criticisms are not true.

2.   When situations arise in which the boy behave badly, explain how their behaviors have affected the class. Require them to stat an appropriate way that the situation could have been handled.

3.   Discuss and model for the boys positive types of criticisms; compare with negative criticisms.

4.   Show films and videotapes where criticisms are true; provide activities by which the boys will show how to use negative criticisms for self-improvement.

E.   The boys will develop confidence in self by actively participating in group and individual activities

1.   Discuss the concept of a family; relate the concept of a family to the class. Provide activities where the boys have to work as a unit.

2.   Assign the boys to teams of four or five, where each team will have a task to complete. Encourage each boy to do his share as a member of the team.

3.   Encourage parents to include the boys in family activities. Give praise when earned as a contributing member of the group.

4.   Provide activities where the boys must assume leadership. Their leadership will determine the success or the failure of the activity.

5.   Provide the boys with situations in which they must make a decision. Give support, guidance, and praise until an appropriate decision is made.

F.   The boys will control their anger when provoked.

1. Use puppets; have the puppets call each other names. Discuss with the boys techniques for ignoring names calling.
2. Provide a system for rewarding and praising the boys when they ignore name calling.
3. Role play situations in which puppets call each other names because of an accidental bump or some other situation. Stress that name calling is unpleasant, but frequently it is best to ignore it.
4. Discuss with the boys that frequently name calling reflects insecurity on the part of the other person, and that the best way of dealing with the problem is to ignore it.

G. They boys will understand the impact of their behaviors upon others.
1. Videotape inappropriate behaviors of the boys. Discuss how these behaviors impact others.
2. Have the boys discuss incidents where negative behaviors have affected them.
3. Role play situations where inappropriate or negative behaviors have caused others to be sad.
4. During the activities in the classroom, encourage the boys to ask if an activity is disturbing to others. Remind the boys to be considerate of others.
5. Develop signals to indicate to the boys that their negative behaviors are affecting others.
6. On bulletin boards, have the boys draw pictures and narrate how positive behaviors impact others.
7. Encourage parents to implement and to follow up strategies at home.

H The boys will understand how drugs may affect social skills development.

1.   Demonstrate the harmful effects that drugs
      have on interpersonal development and
      relationships.
2.   Model how drugs effect interaction with
      others.
3.   Role play how drugs may alter one's
      personality.
4.   Recognize the emotional, mental, and
      physical consequences when drugs are
      misused.
5.   Instruct the boys in the danger of taking
      mind altering drugs.
6.   Have the boys relate how the use of drugs
      can lead to self destruction and isolation
      from family and peers.

General Objectives No. 6 of the Unit:

Young African-American males will use social skills strategies to
solve problems by communicating appropriately with others at home,
community, and school.

Special Objectives:

A.   They boys will practice the art of compromising.
B.   They boys will demonstrate the need to anticipate
      sequences.
C.   The boys will understand the need to set appropriate
      goals.
D.   The boys will develop the skill of looking at
      alternatives.
E.   The boys will know where to find good advice.
F.   The boys will recognize emergency situations.
G.   The boys will demonstrate how to interrupt
      appropriately
H.   The boys will know the relationship between drug
      abuse, HIV, AIDS and STD's.

Recommended Activities: (individualize and expand as
needed)

A.   The boys will practice the art of compromising
      1.   Create situations that offer the boys a chance for
           compromise. Encourage the boys to practice the
           art of compromising provide guidance when
           needed.

2. Demonstrate and model compromises with the boys. Use different occasions and events to demonstrate compromising strategies.

3. Provide activities where the boys have to compromise. Provide guidance and praise to the boys for being cooperative and accepting the compromises.

4. Provide opportunities for the boys to make choices. When choices conflict. Discuss the role of compromising.

B. The boys will demonstrate the need to anticipate consequences.

1. Role play situations in which the consequences of behavior are anticipated by the boys.

2. As the boys participate in instructional activities, encourage them to anticipate the consequences of their behaviors.

3. Read the boys stories, show filmstrips, and have them anticipate the consequences of the characters' behaviors.

4. Provide activities that require the boys to think through behaviors by considering the consequences before reacting.

C. The boys will understand the need to set appropriate goals.

1. Provide time to discuss with the boys the importance of setting realistic goals.

2. Assign activities that will aid the boys in achieving their goals.

3. Initiate and review a variety of techniques to enable the boys to self monitor their activities toward accomplishing their goals.

4. Provide support and encouragement to the boys; praise them frequently.

5. Review films, stories, and videotapes about famous individuals. Have the boys discuss whether or not they thought that these individuals have well-defined goals.

D. The boys will develop the skill of looking at alternatives.

1. Plan activities where the boys are introduced to alternative ways of solving problems.
2. Encourage the boys to "try another way" when their initial approaches do not appear to be working. Provide demonstrations and models for the boys to imitate. Give praise frequently.
3. Role play several situations using alternate approaches to conflict resolutions.

E.   The boys will know where to find good advice.

1. Visit community agencies, such as recreational centers, health clubs, and public libraries. Discuss the purposes and roles of these organizations, pointing out specific services they provide.
2. Invite community individuals to talk with the boys on selected topics. Develop a pool of volunteers to be available for the boys to consult.
3. Role play situations in which the boys are seeking both good and bad advice. Include situations the boys are likely to experience.
4. Place pictures of community helpers on a bulletin board with a description of their duties. Review situations in which the boys may appropriately react with them.

F.   The boys will recognize emergency situations.

1. Discuss with the boys how to avoid emergency situations such as name calling, fighting, stealing, and other aggressive acts. Model and role play several situations.
2. During instructional activities, remind the boys not to interrupt. Praise them for successful attempts.
3. Develop strategies that give the boys clues concerning their time to talk, such as if someone asks a question or stops talking.
4. Role play situations in which the boys are introduced to each other. Encourage them to respond to each other appropriately, to take

turns speaking, and no to interrupt each other.
Praise the boys for their efforts.

H. The boys will know the relationship between drug
abuse, HIV, AIDS, and STD'S.
1. Expand the knowledge HIV, AIDS and STD'S
and their relationship to drug abuse.
2. Demonstrate how to make responsible decisions
concerning controlling specific disease
related to drug abuse.
3. Show films and videos concerning how to
control spreading diseases through drug usage.
4. Draw from experiences of the boys.
5. Invite resource individuals to speak on the
subject.

General Objectives No. 7 of the Unit:

Young African-American males will demonstrate how to experience
positive self-acceptance and awareness.

Specific Objectives:

A. The boys will recognize that changing old habits is
very difficult and requires a systematic plan.
B. The boys will identify individuals who can assist
them in bringing about positive changes.
C. Have the boys to provide a monitoring and follow-up
plan to assist them in making changes.
D. Have the boys to accent the positive things that they
do in the class, have them to praise each other
frequently.
E. Have the boys discuss special traits and
characteristics of each other.
F, The boys will know how drugs effects one's mind.

Recommended Activities: (individualize and expand as
needed)

A. Instruct the boys that changing old habits are very
difficult and requires a systematic plan.
1. Assist the boys in identifying the source of the
problem. Make sure that are able to briefly
describe the problem and explain why they
consider it to be a problem.
2. Instruct students to brainstorm as many solutions
to the problem as they can. A good practice is

for the student to write all the possibilities down.

3. Have students now look through the possibilities and choose   two or three "best" choices.

4. Have the boys discuss how they might arrive at the solution to the problem. Have each boy list the solutions.

5. Develop group activities whereby the group chooses the solution that appears to be the best.

6. Guide the boys in constructing a course of action for changing   old negative habits.

7. Monitor the plan frequently with feedback to the boys.

B. Identify individuals who can assist the boys in bringing about positive changes.

1. Direct the boys to list individuals whom they trust. Have them indicate why they trust these individuals.

2. Expand the discussions by having the boys indicate how selected individuals may help them change negative habits.

3. Review film and videotapes showing famous Black individuals. Ask the boys questions such as:

a. What do you like about the individual?

b. How do you believe these individuals can contribute to bringing about positive change?

c. Do you know anything about the history of this individual?

4. Using the dialogue established in #3, choose two or three famous Black individuals and summarize their histories. Point out how they overcame adverse conditions as well as individuals who assisted them in bringing about positive changes.

5. Discuss with the boys what might have happened if these Black individuals had not changed some of their negative behaviors.

6. Role lay some of the famous Blacks; emphasize how they brought about positive changes.

7. Have the boys develop stories about Blacks who overcame adverse conditions.

C.   Provide a monitoring and follow-up plan to assist the boys in making changes.

1. Develop an evaluation sheet for each boy. Boys indicate daily on the chart progress made toward making changes in their behaviors. (See Appendix E for an example of an evaluation sheet).

2. Check the evaluation sheet weekly and confer individually with each boy, highlighting "positive" and minimizing "negatives".

3. Develop a system for rewarding the boys for keeping their   evaluation sheets in order as well as showing improvement.

4. Teach the boys how to graph their progress for the week by showing the number of each category. Assist them in interpreting what the graphs show.

5. Use role models in the school and community to demonstrate how successful changes can be made.

6. Have a talk show where the boys can relate how they brought about changes.

7. Discuss with the boys factors that should be considered when planning changes.

D.   Accent the positive things that the boys do in the class; praise frequently.

1. Frequently use positive statements about good deeds.

2. Provide opportunities for the boys to discover positive things about themselves through role playing and creative dramatics.

3. Develop a Citizen of the Week Award; stipulate the criteria or standards for achieving the award.

4. Develop activities where all boys can be successful and award them for achieving the success.

5. Have something positive to say about each boy each day.

6. Use the boys as models to assist in shaping positive behaviors.

E. Discuss special traits and characteristics of the boys. Provide opportunities for each boy to record his special traits.

1. Through observations and interviews with the boys and parents, determine special traits and abilities of each boy.

2. Use the knowledge gained from #1 to develop specific activities for the boys to complete. Motivation and success should be high because of the high interest rate.

3. Catch the boys being good and videotape their behaviors with permission from parents. Show and discuss behaviors with the class.

4. Associate videotape of positive behaviors with classroom rules and acts of courtesy.

5. Photograph both negative and positive behaviors with permission from parents. Post photographs on the board under appropriate behaviors or inappropriate behaviors. Discuss ways in which inappropriate behaviors can be made appropriate.

6. Using information from the bulletin board, have the boys role play both types of behaviors.

7. Determine special abilities of the boys as outlined in #1, and assign them special functions, such as setting up and operating the film projector.

F. The boys will know how drugs affects one's mind.

1. Demonstrate to the boys how drugs affect their bodies.

2. Show films and videos on the harmful affects of using drugs.
3. Instruct the boys on the dangers of using steroids.
4. Teach the boys the disadvantages of using tobacco, cigarettes and alcohol.
5. Model how to lead healthy lifestyles.

Evaluation of Social Skills

General evaluation techniques were outlined in chapter 4. If evaluation results are to be effectively used to gauge what extent the stated objectives have been achieved, the evaluation process must be properly planned. First, a decision must be made on what to evaluate. This approach facilitate the selection of appropriate methods and techniques such as:

1. Evaluating the competence of a particular social skill.
2. Determining the baseline behavior for a particular social skill.
3. Using results to revise the curriculum.
4. Providing information to gauge the progress of the boys.
5. Appraising the effectiveness of selected social skills activities.
6. Making sure that the boys demonstrate the necessary pre requisites/skills for performing the social skills.
7. Having the necessary physical and human resources to conduct the unit.
8. Eliciting the cooperation of parents.
9. Providing training for parents to follow up social skills at home.
10. Determining the reactions of the boys toward selected activities.

Informal Evaluation Techniques

Techniques for evaluating the social skills development of young African-American males come in many forms, including formal and informal techniques. Chapter 4 outlined formal techniques. This section will address informal procedures. These techniques are readily accessible or can easily be developed by the classroom teacher. Some recommended strategies include:

1. Develop a brief checklist to assess social skills in a variety of situations.

2. Simulate social activities requiring the boys to portray different roles that can be used to assess their understanding of appropriate behaviors in various settings. Group and individual appraisal of the activity may be conducted by the class.

3. Use group assignments to evaluate the boys' ability to work cooperatively. Record specific incidents, appropriate and inappropriate.

4. Model and provide illustrations of appropriate and inappropriate behaviors. Have the boys demonstrate both types of behaviors and discriminate between them.

5. Structure activities and situations that call for specific kinds of behaviors and observe the performance of the boys. A rating scale may be used.

6. Assess the frequency of inappropriate behaviors; assist the boys in monitoring their own behaviors.

7. With parental permission, use a variety of audio-visual aids such as films and filmstrips depicting appropriate and inappropriate social skills. Have the boys critique what is taking place and give alternative responses.

Table 9.1 Sample Evaluation Checklist for Evaluating Social Skills
Demonstrated Social Skills Competence

GENERAL OBJECTIVES	SPECIFIC Yes No Yes No	PRE- POST-OBJECTIVES
1. Young African-American males will achieve socially acceptable behaviors in social and inter-personal situations.	a. The boys will respect members of the opposite sex.	__ __ __ __
	b. The boys will demonstrate appropriate character traits needed for acceptance in the public.	__ __ __ __
	c. The boys will show respect for the rights and properties of others.	__ __ __ __
	d. The boys will recognize authority and follow instructions of school, home, and the community.	__ __ __ __
	e. The boys will recognize personal roles in public places.	__ __ __ __

Table 9.1 Sample Evaluation Checklist for Evaluating Social Skills
Demonstrated Social Skills Competence (cont'd.)

2. Young African-American males will acquire self-confidence and employ appropriate social skills at home, school, and community	a. The boys will demonstrate how to cope with their feeling and emotions arising from conflicts.	— — — —
	b. The boys will practice acceptable social behaviors at home, school and community.	— — — —
	c. The boys will accept praise when given.	— — — —
	d. The boys will accept criticism when given and demonstrate how to use the information for self-improvement.	— — — —
	e. The boys will develop a sense of price and self-confidence in themselves.	— — — —

Table 9.1 Sample Evaluation Checklist for Evaluating Social Skills
Demonstrated Social Skills Competence (cont'd.)

3. Young African - American males will use social skills strategies to solve problems by communicating appropriately to others at school, home and community.	a. The boys will practice the art of compromising.	— — — —
		— — — —
	b. The boys will demonstrate the need to anticipate consequences.	— — — —
	c. The boys will demonstrate the need to set appropriate goals.	— — — —
	d. The boys will develop the skills of looking at alternatives in making decisions to deny taking drugs and other inappropriate behaviors.	— — — —
	e. The boys will know where to find good advice.	— — — —
	f. The boys will recognize emergency situations.	— — — —
	g. The boys will demonstrate how to interrupt interpersonal behaviors of others, and use assertive behaviors in say no to drugs and other negative behaviors.	— —

Informal evaluation results, such as the Checklist may be used to determine if social intervention is needed as well as grouping boys into different instructional groups to remediate the social deficits the social deficits.

Activities and creative games can be designed to improve social greetings, developing good relationships, respecting the feelings of others, practicing common courtesy, ways to make friends, acceptable ways to show anger, alternative to cursing, learning when an apology is needed, appropriate and inappropriate touching, being a good sport , and the importance o f being a good neighbor. Activities should be age-appropriate. Specific objectives are stated for each area of social skills development, with specific directions and procedures for completing each activity followed by a list of specific questions for children. Desired outcomes are also listed for each activity, an assessment sheet is provided to evaluate social growth. Games and activities may be infused into the curriculum, or common criteria may be developed by the teacher with specific conditions for playing the games. Games and activities may be placed in a learning center or station.

Social skills should not be taught in isolation, but infused throughout the curriculum as needed. Approach and strategies outlined are not meant to be exclusive, Adaptations and modifications are encouraged.

The strategies and intervention reported have been tested with your African-American Males and found to be successful. Results have shown a decrease in negative behaviors and an increase in positive behaviors and achievement. Specific techniques are evaluating the impact of social skills in reducing inappropriate behaviors were comprehensively outlined in chapter 4.   It is recommended that this type of checklist be revised for all of the social skills taught. The checklist or other informal techniques should be administered on a pre-posted basis. Such as procedure permits the teacher to objectively determine to what degree the stated objectives have been achieved and to determine modifications are adaptations needed in the unit.

Summary

In social skills training, young African-American males are taught those skills they must master if they are to become contributing members of society. Emphasis has been placed on developing instructional activities that assist those boys in functioning successfully at school, home, and the community in social situations. Activities have been developed that help the boys control their tempers, initiate compromises, and develop improved interpersonal relationships and strategies for recognizing and respecting authority.

An excellent resource book for promote social skills is Social Skills: Learning to Get Along with Other People.

Chapter 10

Summary

It is commonly thought that young children react to social conflict using different standards than adults. DiMartino's (1990) study refuted this myth, however. His study showed that areas of social conflict in this experiment included: (1) morality, (2) social convention, (3) safety, and (4) institutional rules.

The same premise may be applied to young African-American males, since all children basically precede through the same social developmental stages; however, some young African-American males appear to be at the highest risk for social development. Studies have shown that at-risk young African-American males attained the lowest average on academic achievement scores and were over-represented in categories such as retained students, school dropouts, suspended and expelled students, and referral to special education. These findings confirm that young African-American males are at risk during the early elementary grades.

A significant number of young African-American males are educated in public schools located in urban communities, many of which do not provide good environments in which to educate these boys. Thus, a multitude of problems work against the boys receiving appropriate education. (1) The average young African-American male at risk lives with a single parent whose income is below or at the poverty level. This parent is frequently female. (2) Many young African American males are exposed daily to violence and physical and drug abuse. (3) Many of the boys receive inadequate nutrition and health care. Combined, these factors contribute to many mental, social, and physical problems that impede successful academic and social development.

Holland (1989) summed up the plight of young African-American males by stating that drastic reforms must be made in urban education. Specifically, strategies and interventions must be focused on the individual needs of Black males in the primary grades and must be integrated and coordinated with available community resources.

Many African-American males have developed or adopted alternative ways and styles of coping with problems in their neighborhoods. These behavioral styles are frequently in conflict with the standards of schools and society in general, and may be viewed as negative or destructive. Thus, behavioral styles and models copied and imitated by young African-American males may serve them well in their environments, but are frequently viewed as dysfunctional by the school and society.

Many young African-American males tend to settle differences by physical means. This approach may be attributed to poor impulse control. Also, frequently, they do not accept responsibility for their actions but attribute blame to others for negative and inappropriate behaviors. Generally, young African-American males who are at risk tend to demonstrate lower interpersonal skills compared with other children. It is believed that poor interpersonal skills can be directly attributed to the lack of social skills training during the developmental years.

The value of social skills training for young African-American males has been well documented throughout this text. Social skills training should be considered as an ongoing intervention strategy. Opportunities should be provided in the curriculum for the boys to internalize appropriate behaviors as they develop additional way of interacting with others. Instructional programs must be developed and designed to enable young African-American males to gain knowledge about appropriate interpersonal skills and to employ this newly acquired knowledge in solving their social problems. In order for this goal to be accomplished, young African-American males must be taught effective ways of internalizing their behaviors and assessing how their behaviors affect others.

Teaching appropriate social skills to young African-American males appears to be a promising technique for improving pro-social skills (Taylor, 1992). For example, appropriate social skills are essential for developing personal relationships and accepting the roles of authority figures. Social behaviors are learned; therefore, they can be changed and modified. Proper social skills require that an individual evaluate a situation, choose the appropriate social skills, and perform the social tasks accordingly (Katz, 1991). Unfortunately, many young African-Americans males have not been exposed to appropriate social models or do not possess enough prerequisite skills, such as maturity and self-control, to successfully perform the social skills (Taylor, 1992).

Research findings have clearly demonstrated that diverse groups of children, including young African-American males, are at risk for developing appropriate interpersonal skills. Lack of such skills may lead to feelings of rejection and isolation in classroom settings. There is also ample evidence to suggest that children's social difficulties may emanate from different sources and areas. These deficit areas must be identified and remediated during the early years. Schools must design, direct, and implement intervention programs that permit these young African-American males to experience success (Butler, 1988; Hilliard, 1989; Kagan, 1989; Diggory, 1990; Foster, 1986; Deal, 1990; Holland, 1987; Ayers, 1989).

Studies have consistently shown that negative behaviors are learned behaviors that children imitate from their environments, such as using drugs. Frequently, these hostile and destructive patterns of behavior cannot be controlled by the schools, thus creating conflict and tension between children, parents, and school (Matsueda & Heimer, 1987; Gibbs, 1988).

The preponderance of studies in the area of social learning have consistently shown that the learning styles of some young African-American males are significantly different from those of their peers. Society and the school have failed to capitalize on this salient point. The school has not changed its basic approach to teaching these children over the last several decades, in spite of the vast amount of research and literature on innovative teaching techniques and strategies.

School experiences for young African-American males are usually unrelated to the experiences they bring to school. Their abilities to function satisfactorily in social groups are usually below expected levels set by the school. They have fewer and less rigid control over their impulses and have learned hostile and destructive patterns of behavior as viewed by society and the school. The majority of young African-American males at risk will never become full integrated in society and the school unless early intervention is attempted and social skills are infused and systematically taught throughout the curriculum. It is incumbent upon the school to recognize and accept this fact and to develop strategies to modify, adapt, and gradually promote what is considered to be "appropriate social behavior" through the use of behavior intervention techniques and other strategies.

Personality, temperament, cognitive styles, sociological influences, and ethnic background may all influence the development and learning of young African-American males. The study of social learning theories enables the school to understand both how these boys' cultures can be modified to promote expected learning outcomes and how these boys feel about themselves in relationship to learning. Social skills activities and strategies must be developed to promote the emotional well-being of young African-American males. This approach appears to be in concert with one of the basic premises of this book, which is that a school system that does not deem the teaching of interpersonal skills as important as academic skills may not be preparing its youth for successful democratic participation in our society.

Some observations that appear relevant to educating at risk African-American males and creating effective interpersonal learning strategies include:

1. Seem generally unaware of the "ground rules" for success in school.
2. Are less able to learn from being told than are their counterparts.
3. Are often unable to make simple symbolic interpretations.
4. Tend to have shorter attention spans and consequently have problems with following directions.
5. Are unable to use language in a flexible way.
6. Tend to have little concept of relative size of objects outside their environments.
7. Are less likely to perceive adults as people to whom they can turn for help.
8. Seem to have a low level of curiosity about things.
9. Seem to project a low self-image.
10. Have experiences within a very narrow range.

The difficult part of teaching is not developing appropriate learning strategies for young African-American males, but dealing with the great influx of children who come from emotionally, physically, socially, and financially stressed homes. This is not a school problem alone; society in general must assume the major responsibilities for these environmental atrocities. The school is responsible to the extent that is has not used the vast amount of research and resources to change teaching techniques to educate many young African-American males. For these children, school experiences have virtually remained unchanged for decades. Additionally, teaching techniques are usually unrelated to the experiences they bring to school and do not adequately address the observations outlined. Life in school is mostly teacher-centered, textbook-dominated, restrictive, impersonal, and rigid (Goodland, 1984).

Bridges (1988) summed up the status of education for at-risk African-American males by stating that some models for Black male children's development are broken and we must find solutions to fix them.

These issues and more must be addressed by the school if it is to become responsive to the educational needs of many young African-American males. Policies must be changed at the local, state, and national levels. The Committee for Economic Development (1987) advanced the position that our commitment to the young must go beyond political rhetoric and must produce a well planned curriculum of programs for children from birth through adulthood. This appears to be appropriate for schools to promote in providing equal education opportunities for all children, including young African-American males.

Appendix A

Instructional and Intervention Strategies for Instructing Young African-American Males

List of Recommended Social Skills to be Taught Components of Male Class

I. Bonding
    A. Pledge (first thing in the morning)
    B. Acknowledgment of Unity
        1. Handshake; secret signal; cue; smile.
        2. Words "we are family."
    C. Buddy (Explain to students:)
        1. A buddy can be selected for each unit to work with in the completion of a long-range project.
        2. A buddy you can work with in cooperative learning groups.
        3. A buddy you can share a common interest with (give an interest survey).
        4. A buddy you may eat lunch with, telephone to check over homework with, share a book with, walk with in line.

II Social Skills
    A. Basic Needs
        -   Attention - Allow children to take turns being group learners, readers, student of the day.
        -   Belonging - Given name for the class, special pledge, motto, colors, other symbols that represent belonging.
        -   Importance - We need you today to help us with this task. Your team buddy needs you; your participation is valuable to the group; we are depending on your help. This is your assigned responsibility everyday. Without you, this doesn't operate smoothly. [Biography Board].

- Confidence - Praise; encouragement; present a task that seems to be complex but encourages the student toward mastery.
- Sense of Freedom - (Choices-point out to students:) Even in disciplinary situations; you can either do it now or after school. The choice is yours.
- Fighting - How could you have handled him/her differently? What can I do to help with the problem? What do you feel you would like or need to do now?

B.   Goals (Instruction should be used to foster:)
- Confidence
- Motivation
- Effort
- Responsibility
- Initiative
- Perseverance
- Caring
- Teamwork
- Common sense
- Problem-solving skills.

II   Curriculum

A.   African American Basis
- Infuse topics from Black History Unit
- Use alternative unit approaches for social skills development

B.   Suggested Topics:
- Ancient African kingdoms
- African myths and folklore
- The journey to America
- African/Egyptian math principals
- Slavery
- Famous scientists
- Famous sportsmen
- Famous inventors
- Famous educators
- Famous writers
- Famous entertainers

C. Integrate the buddy system, social skills, oral responses, values and writing, and research organization skills around units.

D. Suggested Other Units
    - Animals
    - Jobs
    - Weather
    - Mysterious phenomena
    - Living things
    - Food

E. Projects
    - Drawings
    - Posters
    - Paper mache

Appendix B

Social Skills To Be Taught

Informal Assessment Inventory

Directions: Check always, sometimes, or never for each statement. There are no correct or incorrect answers.

Aggressions	Always	Sometimes	Never
I get mad often.			
I find other children are friendly to me.			
I get angry when treated unfairly.			
People are always trying to get me.			
I usually hit first.			
I must always protect myself.			
I feel protected.			
I don't get upset if I see something torn or messed up.			
I like fixing broken things.			
People don't hear me unless I talk loud.			
I like to talk loud.			

Organization	Always	Sometimes	Never
I am no good at getting work done.			
I complete tasks easily.			
I remember my books and materials needed for that day.			
I have often lost my lunch ticket.			
I have never lost anything.			
I hang up my coat and put my books away when I arrive home.			
I copy my assignments down and turn them in on time.			
I have trouble finding things in my room.			
It takes time to find papers asked for in my notebook.			

	Always	Sometimes	Never

I have trouble trying to memorize
facts and things.
I remember the words to songs
easily.
I am doing well in school.
Behavior Problems
I get in trouble for many little things.
Nobody pays any attention to me.
I can be happy one minute and
sad the next.
When I see something I need,
I take it.
Other people get me into trouble.
I control my own actions.
I need adults to tell me how to act.
Stress
Sometimes, I feel like running
away.
I don't like to laugh.
It's bad to make a mistake.
It's better to keep your feelings to
yourself.
I like to take risks to grow and
learn.
It is important for me to be the
first in everything.
I like to win at everything.
I don't like for people to touch
me or stand too close to me.
I hate to wait for things.
I get embarrassed easily.

Appendix C

Observation Checklist

Teacher_____ Observer_____
Lesson_____ Date_____ Time_____

	3 Never	2 Frequently	1 Always
Students deals positively with accusations.	_____	_____	_____
Student accepts feelings of others in a nonthreatening manner.	_____	_____	_____
Student respects the feelings of others.	_____	_____	_____
Student knows how to avoid fights and conflicts and display good humor.	--------	----------	----------
Student deals effectively with teasing.	_____	_____	_____
Student moves about room independently to perform routine tasks.	_____	_____	_____
Student stays away from trouble-some situations. Accepts culture values of pupils.	_____	_____	_____
Student verbally shows appreciation when assisted.	_____	_____	_____
Student gives praise or compliments to other students.	_____	_____	_____
Student accepts compliments from others.	_____	_____	_____
Student apologizes for inappropriate behavior.	_____	_____	_____
Student express anger in a positive way.	--------	----------	-----------
Student attempts to understand another's anger without getting angry.	_____	_____	_____
Student shows affection and appreciation toward others.	_____	_____	_____
Student asks permission to borrow or use others' belongings.	_____	_____	_____
Student readily shares objects with others.	_____	_____	_____
Student disagrees in an acceptable manner.	_____	_____	_____
Student accepts losing without becoming upset.	_____	_____	_____
Student does not lose control when left out of group activities.	_____	_____	_____

Appendix D

Cooperative Learning Strategies

Some Cooperative Learning Strategies Circle Activities

Circle activities have been specifically designed to include many different groupings:

Full - The full circle implies that all students would participate in the circle topic and sit together in one circle.

Team - The approach is based on Slavin and Johnson's concepts of cooperative learning (Slavin, 1991; Johnson et al., 1988). Teams consist of five to six students representing different characteristics and abilities. Permanent team assignments are recommended in order to save time assigning teams for each activity.

Recommended strategies for forming cooperative teams include:

Select a name - Team members select a name, take a vote, and then introduce the name to the larger group.

Construct a logo - Members approve of the logo, which will be used as to identify the team. The art teacher may be used as a resource if needed.

Develop a group profile - Provide each team with paper and supplied for designing a group profile on the paper showing each separate individual's interests/strengths/desires onto a team profile chart.

Partner - Provide activities for two students to work together. Students may choose their own partner. After a while, ask students to choose another student whom they do not know as well.

Cooperative Learning Tools

Many of the materials used in circle activities are already accessible in the classroom. Teachers are encouraged to be as creative and innovative as possible.

Puppets - Any puppet that is friendly looking is sufficient. The puppet introduces the circle activities and facilitates the discussion. Students may choose a puppet name or use the name of one of their story characters.

Timer - This can greatly facilitate circle discussions because it lets students know when the circle time is up. Set the timer for the designated time and inform students that when the timer buzzes, the circle is over.

Suggestion box - A small box with a removable top will suffice. Cut a slit ½ by 5" along the top of the box. Have the children decorate the box and write "Suggestions" on the side of big bold letters. Students should be instructed to place their suggestions inside the box. Their suggestions may provide additional circle topics to discuss.

Name cards - Make a set of name cards on 3" x 5" strips of paper. Color code the cards using two colors. Divide the class in half; give the boys alternate colors. Colors may be changed as special events and holidays occur.

Writing book - Make a writing book ditto. Provide space for each student's name in the group. Make several copies of the sheet and staple them between construction paper covers. Use the book during circle time to record students' comments. On selected circles, name the topic at the top of the form and then quickly jot down the main idea of each student's contribution. This is also an incentive for listening.

Recommendations for increasing participation within groups and circles include:

1.   Accent strengths and uniqueness throughout the day. Students won't be able to verbalize their strengths unless they are made aware of them.

2.   Have students keep individual records of their positive self-statements.

3.   Model positive self-statements. If students hear the teacher saying positive comments periodically about themselves, they'll begin to feel it's safe to do so too.

4.   Praise and support students for their use of positive self-statements. Attempt to create an environment that's secure for such growth.

5.   Be supportive of any student who cannot quickly verbalize a positive self-statement in the circle. Use whatever statement is generated and make a positive remark about it; seek approval and endorsement from the student.

6.   Discuss real-life experiences of students in the beginning circles. Students are often more comfortable about sharing things that they have experienced. Invite students to bring something from home of which they are proud or have an interest in.

7.   Invite students to draw a picture of what they will be saying in the circle. This is particularly helpful for shy students. The picture will provide support for the student during discussion.

Appendix E

Sample Evaluation Sheet

Evaluation Sheet (Sample items may be expanded as needed)

	Yes	No	Sometimes
I followed classroom and school rules tody.	___	___	___
I showed respect for others today.	___	___	___
I attempted to control my anger today.	___	___	___
Did I contribute to my group's discussion today?	___	___	___
Did I practice good citizenship habits today?	___	___	___
Was I on my best behavior today?	___	___	___
Was I polite and courteous to my classmates today?	___	___	___
Was I considerate of others today?	___	___	___
Did I use negotiation strategies today?	___	___	___
Did I consider the feelings of others before I responded?	___	___	___
Did I show appreciation for a kind deed today?	___	___	___
I added to my circle of friends today.	___	___	___
I praised classmates for successful tasks completed today.	___	___	___
I recorded my behavior on my performance chart today.	___	___	___

Appendix F

Selected Resources

Films and Filmstrips

Aesop's Fables. Nine color-captioned filmstrips. Educational Projections Corporation. Titles: *The Mean Old Elephant, The Lion and the Goat, The Silly Rabbit, Wolf in Sheep's Clothing, The Loud-Mouthed Frog, The Greedy Dog, The Evil Spider, The Mouse Who Boasted, and The Foolish Donkey.* (1-3).

Animal Stories Series. Six color filmstrips. Educational Reading Service. These filmstrips are made up of photographs of children and their pets and teach responsibility and consideration of others.

Appreciating Our Parents. Color or black/white 16 mm film. Coronet Films. This film is Aesop's fable "one good turn deserves another."

Beginning Responsibility: Being a Good Sport. Color or black/white 16mm film. Coronet Films. Poor Sportsmanship over a checker game leads to a discussion of sportsmanship.

Beginning Responsibility: Learning to Follow Directions. One reel; color or black/white. Coronet. Some of David's toy animals magically come to life and teach him that he must pay attention.

Beginning Responsibility: Lunchroom Manners. Color or black/white 16 mm film. Coronet Films. Through a puppet show, the children in a class realize that clumsiness and impoliteness are funny with Mr. Bungle, but are not desirable among themselves. (1-3).

But It Isn't Yours. Two filmstrips, one 12 inch LP record or cassette, and teacher's guide. Guidance Associates. Two unfinished stories included are these: Part 1, Is it permissible for Bill to keep a dog which has escaped from the pound, Part 2, Is Jeff responsible for returning stolen property that he unknowingly accepted? (K-4).

Conduct and Behavior. Ten color-captioned filmstrips. Educational Projections Corporation. Titles: *In School, On the Playground, On the Street, At Home, Visiting Friends, Traveling, Shopping, In Public Buildings, The Picnic,* and *Responsibility.*

Developing Basic Values. Four color filmstrips and records or cassettes and teacher's guides. Society for Visual Education, Incorporated. Titles: *Respect for Property, Consideration of Others, Acceptance of Others, and Recognition of Responsibilities.*

Fairness for Beginners. Color or black/white 16 mm film. Coronet Films. The film presents the ways of being fair: sharing, taking turns, choosing fairly, and respecting the rights of others.

Getting To Know Me. Four color filmstrips with two records or cassettes and teacher's guide. Society for Visual Education. The film is designed to develop self-understanding and self-acceptance. Titles: *People Are Like Rainbows, A Boat Named George, Listen! Jimmy!,* and *Strike Three! You're In.*

Good Citizens. Encyclopedia Britannica Educational Corporation, 1961. The file discusses courtesy, cooperation, dependability, and fair play.

Good Manners. Series of six filmstrips (average 48 frames each). Encyclopedia Britannica Educational Corporation. Good manners are presented as a means of getting along with people.

Guidance Stories, Series No. 8490. Six color filmstrips. Encyclopedia Britannica Educational Corporation. Titles: *Sharing With Others, Playing Fair, Sticking to Your Job, New Friends - Good Friends, One Kind of Bravery,* and *Taking Care of Your Things.*

Late for Dinner: Was Dawn Right? Color or black/white 16 mm film. Encyclopedia Britannica Educational Corporation. An open-ended film shows that conflicting feelings are normal.

Little Citizens Series. Society for Visual Education, 1960. The film highlights students' responsibilities toward others.

Little Things That Count. Eight color filmstrips with four records or cassette Teach-A-Tapes and teacher's manual. Eye Gate House. Freedom's Foundation Awards Winner. The stories involve the joy of helping others, honesty, perseverance, responsibility, justice, reverence, and love.

Minorities and Majorities. Six color filmstrips with three cassette Teach-A-Tapes and teacher's manual. Eye Gate House. The film deals with child-to-child prejudice, being part of a group, being outside of the group, and being within a group. Ethnic, national, religious, and color distinctions are not discussed as issues.

Practicing Good Citizenship. Six filmstrips; individual filmstrips also available. Troll Associates, 1972. Film titles: *Growing Up To Be A Good Citizen; When To Be A Leader, When To Be A*

Follower; Recognizing Individual Differences; A Good Citizen In School;

Be A Danger Fighter; and *A Newcomer Comes To Town*.
Tales of the Wise Old Owl. Filmstrips and records in three
groups. Society for Visual Education. Group 1: *Dr. Retriever's Surprise
and Silly Excuses*. Group 2: *Bushy the Squirrel and Peggy the Pup*.
Group 3: *The Feather That Was Lost and Pearl of Great Price*.
    Teaching Children Values Through Unfinished Stories. Two
color filmstrips, one 33 1/3 rpm record or cassette, and teacher's guide.
Educational Activities, Inc. Open-ended stories enable the pupil to
identify with the central character and to think about and devise solutions
to problems offered.
    That's Not Fair. Two filmstrips with record or cassette.
Guidance Associates. Part 1: Is it fair to take another's place in a gift line?
Part 2: Two boys return some lost spectacles and are undecided about
how to share the reward, which is a watch.
    The Ant and The Dove. Color or black/white 16 mm film.
Coronet Films. This film is Aesop's fable, "One good turn deserves
another."
    The "Be Kind" Stories. Four color filmstrips with two cassette
Teach-A-Tapes and teacher's manual; coloring books available. Eye Gate
House. The emphasis is on expressing more kindness in everyday living.
    The Lemonade Stand: What's Fair? Color or black/white 16 mm
film. Encyclopedia Britannica Educational Corporation. Focuses on the
meaning of commitment, obligations, and responsibility to others.
    The Picture Life of Thurgood Marshall. Young, M. B. Watts,
1971. A brief biography of the Black lawyer who fights for the rights of
African-American citizens and eventually becomes the first Black man to
become an Associate Justice of the Supreme Court.
    The Report Card: How Does Ricardo Feel? Color or black/white
16 mm film. Encyclopedia Britannica Educational Corporation. The film
teaches that when individuals do not control their emotions, anger can be
destructive.
    Values. Six color filmstrips with three cassette Teach-A-Tapes or
filmstrips with cassettes. Eye Gate House, 1972. Film titles: *Telling
the Truth, What Is Stealing?, Kindness, Politeness, Responsibility*, and
Citizenship. This film is designed to help the student develop a standard
of values; both appropriate and inappropriate responses to a conflict
situation are given without a judgement being made. By discussing or

role playing each problem and response, students can develop their own
answers and formulate their own set of values.
    Ways To Settle Disputes. One reel, color or black/white.

Collaborator: Carter Davidson. The film emphasizes that settlement of conflict must be desired to be effective and gives four ways of settling disputes.

What Do You Expect Of Others? Three filmstrips, one 12-inch LP record or cassette, and teacher's guide. Guidance Associates. The film helps children learn that what you expect a person to be like has much to do with how he or she acts toward you.

What Happens Between People? Two filmstrips, one 12-inch LP record or cassette, and teacher's guide. Guidance Associates. The film assists children in becoming aware of types of human interactions between individuals and groups.

You Got Mad: Are You Glad? Two filmstrips, one 12-inch LP record or cassette, and teacher's guide. Guidance Associates. The film helps children discover the cause and effects of hostility, stressing behavioral choices such as mediation, third-party judgment, and compromise as ways to resolve conflicts.

Yours, Mine, and Ours. Color or black/white 16 mm film. Encyclopedia Britannica Educational Corporation. Reflects classroom situations showing proper responsibility for ownership; teaches children to recognize group and individual responsibilities.

Records

Aesop's Fables. 12-inch LP record. Caedman (Alesco). Boris Karoff reads 42 classical moral and ethical tales. (1-6).

American Poems of Patriotism. 12-inch LP record. Caedman (Alesco). Nineteen selections are read by Ed Begley, Julie Harris, and Frederick O'Neal.

Living With Others - Citizenship I, II. Six records or tape cassettes. Society for Visual Education, Incorporated. Subjects include: Bad example of others, cheating, breaking family rules, stealing, lost friendships, safety, etc.

Filmloops

Understanding Ourselves and Others. Five filmloops. Educational Reading Service. Titles: *Understanding the Difference Between Alone and Lonely; Fear - Real and Imaginary; Why We Get Angry; People Are Different, Aren't They?* and *Learning When and Where.*

Endnotes

Chapter 3

Specific directions for conducting a skillstreaming program may be
found in Goldstein, A. and McGinnis, E. (1984).
*Skillstreaming the
elementary child.* Chicago, IL: Research Press Company.

Chapter 5

1 N. G. Hoffman, P. A. Harrison, & C. A. Belile. (1986). Alocholics
Anonymous After Treatment, Attendance, and Abstinence.
Journal of Addiction, 218, 311-318.

2 N. S. Miller & J. Chappel. (1991). History of Disease Concept.
PsychiatricAnnals, 21 (2), 1-8.

Chapter 7

An excellent book to review for involving African-American Mothers
in the Schools is Winters, G. (1993). African-American
Mothers and Urban Schools. New York: Lexington Books.

Glossary

Abuse - Use of a drug for non-medical purposes which results in health or social problems.

Addiction - Usually refers to dependence, compulsive, chaotic use.

Aggression - An attempt to physically harm someone

Anger - A defensive emotional reaction that occur when one is frustrated, denied, or attached.

Assessment - A process of collecting formal and informal data about pupils for the purpose of making instructional decisions.

Anxiety - A feeling that exists when one is afraid but can not recognize the cause.

Behavioral deficit - A response that is a problem because there has been few opportunities to practice the behavior.

Behavioral description - A statement that includes a description of specific behaviors being observed.

Behavioral objective - A form for writing an instructional objective that emphasizes expected students outcomes, types of evaluation, and performance standards.

Communication - A message sent by a student with the planned intention of affecting another student's behavior.

Compromising - Giving up one's goal while the other student does the same in order to reach an agreement.

Conformity - Changes in behavior that results from group influences, yielding to group pressure when no direct request has been made.

Dependence - Habituation, compulsive use, psychological or physical need for drugs, drug seeking despite consequences of use.

Drug Abuse - Substance taken in any way that alter mood, perception, or brain function, from prescribed drugs to alcohol to solvents.

Effective Communication When the students' message is interpreted in the same way it was intended.

Fear - Real or imaginary feelings shown by students, resulting in physiological response.

Identify - A consistent set of attitudes that describe, characterize and define who one is.

Imaginary - Feelings or experiences that exist only in the imagination or fantasy, not real experiences.

Integration - Combining several concepts, practices, approaches, methods, etc., into one idea or expression.

Intentions - Planned, deliberated, and conscience acts to satisfy immediate goals.

Internalized Behavior - Intrinsic motivation which occurs when students behave appropriately because the behavior bring them personal satisfaction.

Interpersonal Communication Skills - Skills that promote honest communication and positive attitudes among individuals.

Modeling - A term used in social learning theory to describe how students learn as a result of observing and imitating others.

Negotiation - A process by which students who have opposite views and interests attempt to come to an agreement.

Observation - A procedure in which the observer watches and records behaviors of individuals.

Positive Reinforcement - Presenting a reward, or some object that will increase positive or appropriate behaviors of pupils.

Praise - Positive verbal and nonverbal statements made by teachers to strengthen appropriate student behaviors.

Reinforcements - Rewards given for students demonstrating appropriate behaviors to increase the possibilities of those behaviors being repeated.

Rewards - Reinforcers, tangible and intangible objects, given to students to strengthen appropriate behaviors.

Self-Acceptance - Pride in yourself, or a high regard for yourself.

Social Skills Training - A structured intervention design to assist students in improving interpersonal skills.

Self-Evaluation - A students estimation of how positively their behaviors, manner, and actions compare with their peers.

Social Interaction - A common bond linking two or more students together.

Task Analysis - A process for breaking down complex tasks into two small manageable steps so that they can be successfully completed one at a time.

Tolerance - Equal adaptation, which is the body/brain's attempt to establish homeostasis in the presence of a substance.

Withdrawal - Physical or psychological symptoms appear when the drug is discontinued.

Bibliography

Abell Salutes. (1991).*Education Opportunity Program (EOP) at Lake Clifton-Eastern Senior High.* The Abell Report, 4, 1.

Adams, D. N. (1990). Involving students in cooperative learning. *Teaching Pre K-8,* 20, 51-52

Allen, B. B. (1990). *Cooperative learning workshop.* Hebbville elementary school. Baltimore, MD: Baltimore County Schools.

Anita, S., G., & Kreimeyer, K. (1992). *Project Interact. Interventions for social integration of young hearing-impaired children.* Washington, DC: Office of Special Education and Rehabilitative Services.

Ascher, C. (1991). *School programs for African-American males.* Eric Document Reproduction Services. ED 334340.

Athanases, S. Z. (1993). Adapting and tailoring lessons: Fostering teacher reflection to meet varied students' needs. *Teacher Education Quarterly,* 20, 1, 71-81

Ayers, W. (1989). Childhood at risk. *Educational Leadership,* 46, 8, 7-72

Bailey, R. C., Hser, Y., Hsieh, S., & Anglin, M. D. (1994). Influences affecting maintenance and cessation of narcotics addiction. Special Issues: Drugs and crime revisited. *Journal of Drug Issues,* 24 (1-2), 249-272.

Bandura, A. (1977). *A social learning theory.* Englewood Cliffs, NJ: Prentice-Hall.

Bandura, A., & Walters, R. (1963). *Social learning and personality development.* New York: Holt, Rinehart, and Winston.

Bank, J. A. (1991). Multicultural education: For freedom's sake. *Educational Leadership,* 49,(4), 22-35.

Bankee, N. C., & Obiakor, F. E. (1992). Educating the Black male: Renewed imperatives for Black and white communities. *Scholar and Educator: The Journal of the Society of Educators and Scholars,* 15 (2), 16-31.

Barth, R. (1990). *Improving schools from within.* San Francisco: Jossey-Bass, Inc.

Beane, J. A. (1990). *A middle school curriculum: From rhetoric to reality.* Columbus, OH: National Middle School Association.

Beane, J. A. (1993). The search for a middle school curriculum. *School Administrator,* 50 (3), 8-14.

Beck, A. J., & Mamola, C. J. (1998). *Prisoners in 1998.* Bureau of Justice Statistics, U S. Department of Justice

Bennett, C. (1986). *Comprehensive multicultural education. Theory and Practice.* Boston: Allyn and Bacon.

Berry, G. L., & Asamen, J. K. (Eds.). (1989). *Black students: Psychosocial issues and academic achievement.* Newbury Park, CA: Corwin Press.

Bert, C. R. G., & Bert, M. (1992). *The Native American: An exceptionality in education and counseling.* (ERIC Document Reproduction Service, No. Ed 351168) Clearinghouse on Rural Education and Small Schools, Charleston, West Virginia.

Bigelow, G. E., Brooner, R. K., & Silverman, K. (1999). Drug reinforcement vs non-drug reinforcement. *Journal of Psychopharmacology*, 12 (1), 8-14.

Bilken, R. (1990). Making differences ordinary. In W. Stainback & M. Forest (Eds.), *Educating all children in the mainstream of regular education.* Baltimore, MD: Paul H. Brooks.

Blake, B. G. (1967). A follow up of alcoholics treated by behavior therapy. *Behavior Research and Therapy*, 15, 89-94.

Boland, F. J., Mellor, C. S., & Revasky, S. (1978). Chemical aversion treatment of alcoholism: Lithium as the aversive agent. *Behavior Research and Therapy*, 16, 401-409.

Botvin, G. J., Schinke, S., & Orlandi, M. A. (Eds.). (1995). *Drug abuse prevention with multiethnic youth.* Thousand Oaks, CA: Sage publication.

Bowman, B. (1994). *Cultural diversity and academic achievement.* Oak Brook, IL: North Central Regional Educational Laboratory.

Bridges, R. E. (1988). *Black male child development: A broken model.* Paper presented at the 120th Annual Convention, American Association of School Administrators, Las Vegas, Nevada.

Brody, G., & Stoneman, Z. (1977). Social competencies in the developmentally disabled: Some suggestions for research and training. *Mental Retardation*, 15 (4), 41-43.

Brofenbrenner, V. (1979). *The ecology of human development.* Cambridge, MA: Harvard University Press.

Brown, J. (1991, June 12). Coleman school's all-male class a success. *The Baltimore Sun*, Section D, pp 1-3.

Brown, J. H. (1995). *Turning out and turning on: Student response to contemporary drug education*, Audiotape of Seminar Presentation, New York: Lindesmith Center.

Brown, J. H., & Horowitz, J. E. (1993). Deviance and deviants: Why adolescent substance use prevention programs do not work. *Evaluation Review*, 17 (5), 529-555.

Brown J. H. (1997). Listen to the kids. *American School Board Journal*, 184, 38-47.

Bureau of Justice Statistics. (2002). *Criminal offenders statistics*. U. S. Department of Justice. Online: http://www.oj[/usdoj/gov/bjs/crimoff.htm

Butler, K. (1988). How kids learn: What theorists say. *Learning Styles*, 30-34.

Butler, O. B. (1989). Early help for kids at-risk: Our nation's best investment. *NEA Today*, 7 (6), 51-53.

Cahalan, M. W. (1986). *Historical corrections statistics in the United States, 1850-1984*. Bureau of Justice Statistics, U. S. Department of Justice.

Caliguri, J. P. (1992). Drug education in the schools: Does it have a future? *Journal of Alcohol and Drug Education*, 37 (3), 17-22.

Cassidy, E. (1988). *Reaching and involving Black parents of handicapped children in their child's education program*. Lansing, MI: Cause, Inc. (ERIC Document Reproduction Service No. Ed. 302982).

Chaney, E. F., O'Leary, M.R., & Marlatt, G. A. (1978). Skill training with alcoholic. *Journal of Consulting and Clinical Psychological*, 46, 1092-1104.

Chassin, L. (1984). *Adolescent substance use and abuse. Advances in Child Behavioral Analysis and Therapy*, 3, 99-152.

Chiricos, T. G. (1994). *Moral panic as ideology: Race, drugs, violence, and prisons in the U. S. School Criminology and Criminal Justice*. Florida State University, Tallahassee. Paper presented at the Annual Meeting of the International Sociological Association.

Clark, M. L. (1991). Social identity, peer relations, and academic competence of African American adolescents. *Education and Urban Society*, 24 (1), 41-52.

Collins, T. W., & Hatch, J. A. (1992). Supporting the social-emotional growth of young children. *Dimensions of Early Childhood*, 21, 17-21.

Committee for Economic Development. (1987). *Children in need: Investment strategies for the educationally disadvantaged*. New York: Holt, Rinehart, & Winston.

Cummins, J. (1984). *Bilingual and special education: Issues in assessment pedagogy*. San Diego: College-Hill Press.

Dalli, C. (1991). *Scripts for children's lives: What do parents and early childhood teachers contribute to children's understanding of events in their lives.* (ERIC Document Reproduction Service No. Ed. 344664).

Deal, T. E. (1990). Reforming reform. *Educational Leadership,* 47 (8), 6-12.

Delgado-Gaitan, C. (1991). Involving parents in the schools: A process of empowerment. *American Journal of Education,* 100, 20-46.

DeWitt, P. E. (1994). The crucial early years. *Time Magazine,* 143 (16), 68.

Diggory, S. F. (1990). *According to schooling: The Developing child.* Cambridge, MA: Harvard University Press.

DiMartino, E. C. (1990). The remarkable social competence of young children. *International Journal of Early Childhood,* 22, 23-31.

Dodge, D. T. (1988). *The creative curriculum for early childhood.* Washington, DC: Creative Associates International.

Dorr-Bremme, D. W. (1992). *Discourse and social identity in a kindergarten-first grade classroom.* (ERIC Document Reproduction Service No. Ed. 352111).

Dusenbury, L., Lake, A., & Falco, M. (1997). A review of the evaluation of 47 drug abuse prevention curricula available nationally. *Journal of School Health,* 67 (4), 127-132.

Eisner, E. (1991). What really counts in school? *Educational Leadership,* 10-17.

Ellickson, P. L., Bell, R. M., & McGuigan, K. (1993). Preventing adolescent drug use: Long-term results of a junior high program. *American Journal of Public Health,* 83 (6), 856-861.

Elliot, J. (1995). Drug prevention placebo: How DARE wastes time, money, and police. *Reason,* 14-21.

Erikson, E. H. (1959). *Identity and the life cycle.* In Psychological Issues Monograph, I. New York: International Universities Press.

Evans, A., & Bosworth, K. (1997). Building effective drug programs. *Research Bulletin* No. 19. Phi Delta Kappa Center for Evaluation and Research.

Finders, M., & Lewis, C. (1994). Why some parents don't come to school. *Educational Leadership,* 51, (8), 50-54.

Forest, M. (1990). *MAPS and cities.* Presentation at Peak Parent Center Workshop. Colorado Springs, CO.

Foster, H. L. (1986). *Jivin and playin the dozens. In the persistent dilemma in our schools* (2nd ed.). Cambridge, MA: Ballinger Publishing Company.

Furnham, A. (1986). Social skills training with adolescents and young adults. In C. R. Hollins & P. Trower (Eds.), *Handbook of social training*, 1, 33-57. Oxford: Pergamon.

Gaeddert, W. P. (1983). *Role model choice: Who do women say their models are?* Detroit: Annual Meeting of the Midwestern Psychological Association.

Gallagher, J. J. (1989). *The impact of policies for handicapped children on future early education policy*. Phi Delta Kappa, 121-124.

Gibbs, C. R. (1991). Project 2000: Why Black men should teach Black boys. *Dollars and Sense*, February/March, 19-29.

Gibbs, J. T. (1988). *Young, Black, and male in America: An endangered species*. Dover, MA: Auburn House Publishing Company.

Gill, W. (1991). Jewish day schools and African-American youth. *Journal of Negro Education*, 60 (4) 566-580.

Glover, J. H., & McCue, P.A. (1977). Electrical aversion therapy with alcoholics: A comparative follow-up study. *British Journal of Psychiatry*, 130, 279-286.

Goode, E. (1989). *Drugs in American society*. New York: McGraw-Hill.

Goodlad, J. L. (1984). A place called school. New York: McGraw-Hill.

Goodstadt, M. (1989). Drug education: The prevention issues. *Journal of Drug Education*, 19 (3), 1977-208.

Gordon, E. T., Gordon, E. W., & Nembhard, J. G. (1995). Social science literature concerning African American men. Special Issue: Pedagogical and contextual issues affecting African American males in school and society. *Journal of Negro Education*, 63 (4), 508-531.

Graham, P. G. (1987). Black teachers: A drastically scarce resource. Phi Delta Kappa, 68, 598-605.

Greenwood, P. (1992). Substance abuse among high-risk youth and potential intervention. *Crime and Delinquency*, 38 (4), 444-458.

Gregorc, A. F. (1993). *An adult guide to style: The Gregorc-Style Delineator*. Columbia, CT: Gregorc Associates, Inc.

Gresham, F. M. (1985). Utility of cognitive-behavioral procedures for social skills training with children: Critical review. *Journal of Abnormal Child Psychology*, 13, 423-491.

Gresham, F. M., & Elliott, S. N. (1989). Social skills deficits as a primary learning disability. *Journal of Learning Disabilities*, 22 (2), 120-124

Grob, C., & DeRios, M. D. (1992). Adolescent drug use in cross-cultural perspective. *The Journal of Drug Issues*, 22 (1), 126-139.

Gruenewald, L. J., & Pollok, S. A. (1990). Language interaction in curriculum and instruction: *What the classroom teacher needs to know*. Austin, TX: Pro-Ed.

Haltiwanger, J. (1992). *A normative study of development in context: Growth toward independence in social function skills of young children.* Clearinghouse on Teacher Education. (ERIC Document Reproduction Service No. Ed. 342504). Washington, DC.

Hamburg, D. A. (1992). *A decent start: Promoting healthy child development in the first three years of life.* Clearinghouse on Teacher Education. (ERIC Document Reproduction Service No. Ed. 338431). Washington, DC.

Harris, S. M. (1992). Black male masculinity and same-sex friendship. Western *Journal of Black Studies*, 16, 74-81.

Harry, B., Allen, N., & McLaughlin, M. (1992). *Communication versus compliance: Working with African-American parents in special education.* Paper presented at the Annual Meeting of the American Education Research Association, San Francisco.

Hatch, T., & Gardner, H. (1988). How kids learn: What scientists say: New research on intelligence. *Learning*, 37.

Hedley, C., Houtz, J., & Baratta, A. (1990). *Cognition, curriculum, and literacy.*Norwood, NJ: Ablex Publishing Company.

Higgins, S. T., & Silverman, K. (1999). *Motivating behavior change among illicit drug abusers: Research on contingency management interventions.* Washington, DC: American Psychological Association.

Hilliard, A. G. (1988). Conceptual confusion and the persistence of group oppression through education. *Journal of Equity and Excellence*, 24 (1), 36-43.

Hilliard, A. G. (1989). Teachers and cultural styles in a pluralistic society. *NEA Today,* 7 (6), 65-69.

Holland, S. (1987). A radical approach to educating Black males. *Education Week, Commentary*, 24-25.

Holland, S. (1991). *Why Black men should teach Black boys. Project 2000.* Baltimore, MD: A report to the Baltimore City Public Schools.

Holland, S. (1992). Same gender classes in Baltimore: How to avoid problems faced in Detroit, Milwaukee. *Journal of Equity and Excellence*, 25 (2) 4-93.

Horan, J. J., Rude, S. S., & Keillor, R. M. (1999). *Handbook of prescriptive treatments for children and adolescents* (2nd ed.). In

Ammerman, Robert T. (Ed). Hersen, Michael (Ed.) et al. Boston: Allyn and Bacon.

Horowitz, R., & Pottieger, A. E. (1991). Gender bias in juvenile justice handling of seriously crime-involved youths. *Journal of Research in Crime and Delinquency*, 28 (1), 75-100.

Hudley, C. A. (1992). *The reduction of peer directed aggression among highly aggressive African-American boys.* Clearinghouse on Teacher Education. (ERIC Document Reproduction Service No. Ed. 346203.) Washington, DC.

Hudley, C. A. (1993). An attributional intervention to reduce peer-directed aggression among African-American boys. *Child Development*, 64, 124-138.

Hutchinson, E. O. C. (1999). *The crisis in Black and Black-Afrocetric news.* Middle passage press (http:/www.afrocentricnews.com/html/ofaricrimal.html)

Ingrassia. M. (1993). Endangered family. *Newsweek*, 122, 17-19.

Irvine, J. J. (1989). Beyond role models: An examination of cultural influences on the pedagogical perspectives of Black teachers. *Peabody Journal of Education*, 66 (4), 218-226.

Jackson, T. R., & Smith, J. W. (1978). A comparison of two aversion treatment methods of alcoholism. *Journal of Studies on Alcohol*, 39, 187-191.

Jewett, J. (1992). *Aggression and cooperation: Helping young children develop constructive strategies.* Clearinghouse on Teacher Education. (ERIC Document Reproduction Service No. Ed. 351147).

Johnson, D. W., Johnson, R., & Holubec, E. (1988). *Cooperation in the classroom.* Edina, MN: Interaction Book Company.

Johnson, L. D., O'Malley, P. M., & Bachman, J. G. (1998). *National survey results on drug use for monitoring the future study.* Rockville, MD: U. S. Department of Health and Human Services.

Johnson, W., & Johnson, R. (1990). Social skills for successful group work. *Educational Leadership*, 47 (4), 29-33.

Kagan, S. L. (1989). *Early care and education: Beyond the schoolhouse doors.* Phi Delta Kappa, 107-112.

Kagan, S. L. (1990). The structural approach to cooperative learning. *Educational Leadership*, 47 (4), 12-15.

Kandel, M., & Kandel, E. (1994). Flight of memory. *Discover Magazine*, 32-38.

Katz, L. G. (1991). *The teacher's role in social development of young children.* Urbana Illinois Clearinghouse on Elementary and Early

Childhood Education (ERIC Document Reproduction Service No. ED 331642).

Keller, D., & Dermatis, H. (1999). Current status of professional training in the addictions. *Substance Abuse*, 20 (3), 123-140.

Klein, S., Petersilla, J., & Turner, S. (1990). Race and imprisonment decisions in California. *Science*, 247 (4944), 812-816.

Kristo, J. V., & Health, P. A. (1982). *Today's curriculum: An integrative approach*. Washington, DC: University of America Press.

Kunjufu, J. C. (1984). *Developing positive self-images and discipline in Black children*. Chicago: African American Images.

Lane, P. S., & McWhirter, J. J. (1992). A peer mediation model: Conflict resolution for elementary and middle school children. *Elementary School Guidance and Counseling*, 27, 15-21.

LaPoint, V. (1992). Accepting community responsibility for African American youth education and socialization. *Journal of Negro Education*, 61 (4), 451-454.

Lareau, A. (1987). Social class differences in family school relationships: The importance of cultural capital. *Sociology of Education*, 60, 73-85.

Levine, E. M., & Kozak, C. (1979). Drug and alcohol use, delinquency, and vandalism among middle class pre-and post-adolescents. *Journal of Youth and Adolescence*, 8 (1), 91-101.

Lloyd, D. N. (1978). Prediction of school failure from third grade data. *Educational and Psychological Measurement*, 38 (4), 193-200.

Lutfiyya, Z. (1988). *Reflections and relationships between people with disabilities and typical people*. Syracuse, NY: Syracuse University, Center on Human Policy.

Lutfiyya, Z. (1991). *Tony Santi and the bakery: The roles of facilitation, accommodation, and interpretation*. Syracuse, NY: Syracuse University, Center on Human Policy.

Lynam, D. R., Milich, R., Zimmerman, R., Novak, S. P., Logan, T. K., Martin, C., Leukefeld, C., & Clayton, R. L. (1999). Project DARE: No effects at 10 Year Follow Up. *Journal of Consulting and Clinical Psychology*, 76 (4), 590-593.

Lynch, E. W., & Stein, R. (1987). Parent participation by ethnicity: A comparison of Hispanic, Black, and Anglo families. *Exceptional Children*, 54, 105-111.

Mancus, S. M. (1992). Influence of male teachers on elementary school children's stereotyping of teacher competence. *Sex Roles*, 26 (3), 109-126.

Mansbach, S. C. (1993). We must put family literacy on the national agenda. *Reading Today*, 37.

Manwar, A. (1997). *Social construction of "self" among the New York City crack dealers.* National Development and Research Institutes, Inc. New York. Paper presented at a meeting of the Society for the Study of Social Problems.

Marion, R. (1981). *Educators, parents, and exceptional children.* Rockville, MD:Aspen.

Marlatt, G. A. (1973). *A comparison of aversive conditioning procedures in the treatment of alcoholism.* A paper presented at the Annual Meeting of the Western Psychological Association, Anaheim, CA.

Martin, C. E., Duncan, D. F., & Zunich, E. M. (1983). Students' motives for discontinuing illicit drug taken. *Health Values: Achieving High Level Wellness*, 7 (5) 8-11.

Matsueda, R. L., & Heimer, K. (1987). Race, family, structure, and delinquency: A test differential association and social control theories. *American Sociology Review*, 54 (6), 826-840.

Mauer, M., & Huling, T. (1995). *Young Black Americans and the criminal justice system: Five years later.* The Sentencing Project (http://www.sentencing project.org/policy 19070.htm).McGinnis, E., & Goldstein, A. (1984). Skill streaming the elementary child. IL: Research Press Company.

McRae, L. (1994). *The need for African-American male teachers as role models.* Unpublished Master's Thesis: Coppin State College.

Meyer, C. K. (1992). An analysis of factors related to robbery-associated assaults on police officers. IL: *Journal of Police Science and Administration*, 10 (2), 127-150.

Miller, S., & Chappel, J. (1991). History of disease concept. *Psychiatric Annuals*, 21 (12, 1-8.

Miller, W. R., Hendrick, K. A., & Taylor, C. A. (1983) Addictive behavior and life problems before and after behavioral treatment of problem drinkers. *Addictive Behaviors*, 8, 403-412.

Moll, I. (1991). *The material and social in Vygotsky's theory of cognitive development.* Clearinghouse on Teacher Education. (ERIC Document Reproduction Service No. Ed. 346988). Washington, DC.

National Correction Reporting Program. (1996). Bureau of Justice Statistics. Washington, DC: U. S. Department of Justice.

Newcomb, M., & Bentler, P. (1988). *Consequences of adolescent drug use: Impact on the lives of young adults.* Newbury Park, CA: Sage Publications.

Newman, C. F., & Ratto, C. (1999). Thinking your way clean: Rational emotive behavior therapy with a poly-substance abuser. In Dowd, E. T., and Rugle, L. *Comparative treatment of substance abuse.* New York: Springer Publishing Company.

Obiakor, F. E. (1990). Development of self-concept: Impact on student's learning. *The Journal of the Southeastern Association of Educational Opportunity Program Personnel,* 9 (1), 16-33.

Obiakor, F. E. (1991). Self-concept: Impact on Black students' learning. *SENGA,* 1 (2) 48-53.

Obiakor, F. E. (1992). Self-concept of African-American students: An operational model for special education. *Exceptional Children,* 59, (2), 160-167.

O'Brien, J., & O'Brien, C. (1991). *Members of each other - perspectives on social support for people with severe disabilities.* Lithuania, GA: Responsive Systems Associates.

O'Brien, L. (1989). *Learning styles make the student aware.* NASSP Bulletin, October, 85-89.

O'Connor, J., & Saunders, B. C. (1992). Drug education: An appraisal of the popular preventive. *The International Journal of Addictions,* 27 (2), 165-185.

Odom, S., & McEvoy, M. (1988). Integration of young children with handicapped and non-handicapped children: Mainstreamed versus integrated special education. In S. Odom & M. Karnes (Eds.), *Early Intervention for Infants and Children with Handicaps: An Empirical Base* (pp. 241-267). Baltimore, MD: Paul H. Brooks.

Oei, T. P. S., & Jackson, P. (1980). Long-term effects of group and individual social skills training with alcoholics. *Addictive Behavior,* 5, 129-136.

O'Farrell, T. J., & Feehan, M. (1999). Alcoholism treatment and the family: Do family and individual treatment for alcoholic adults have preventive effects for children? *Journal of Studies on Alcohol,* 13, 125-129.

Oswald, D. P., & Sinah-Nirbay, N. (1992). Current research on social behavior. *Behavior Modification,* 16 (4), 443-447.

Owens, S. J. (1991). *Establishing staff training for identifying learning styles in the preschool setting.* (ERIC Document Reproduction Service No. Ed. 342501).

Palermo, G. B., & Simpson, D. (1994). At the roots of violence: The progressive decline and dissolution of the family: *International Journal of Offender Therapy and Comparative Criminology*, 38 (2), 105-116.

Pandey, S., & Coulton, C. (1994). Unraveling neighborhood change using two-wave panel analysis. A case study of Cleveland in the 1980s. *Social Work Research,* 18 (2), 83-96.

Peck, C. A., & Cooke, T. P. (1983). Benefits of mainstreaming at the early childhood level: How much can we expect? *Analysis and intervention in developmental disabilities*, 3, 1-22.

Peele, S. (1996). *Don't panic! A parent's guide to understanding and preventing alcohol and drug abuse.* New York: The Linde Smith Center.

Ponton, L. (1997). *The romance of risk: Why teenagers do the things they do?* New York: Basic Books.

Poplin, M. S. (1988). Holistic/constructivist principles of the teaching/ learning process: Implications for the field of learning disabilities. *Journal of Learning Disabilities*, 21 (7), 410-416.

Prince, T. J. (1990). *Community service project at Morehouse College targeted to at-risk youth.* Draft. Atlantic: Morehouse College Counseling Center.

Project 2000 Teacher Assistant Orientation. *Center for educating African-American males.* School of Education and Urban Studies. Morgan State University, Baltimore, MD.

Rancifer, J. L. (1991). *Restructuring teacher education: Effective strategies to increase the number of Black students in education programs.* Association of Teacher Education, Washington, DC.

Reynolds, J., & Gerstein, M. (1992). Learning style characteristics: An introductory workshop. *Clearinghouse on Teacher Education,* 66 (2), 122-126.

Rizzo, J. V., & Zabel, R. H. (1988). *Educating children and adolescents with behavioral disorders: An integrative approach.* Boston: Allyn and Bacon.

Rosenbaum, M. (1999). *Safety first: A reality-based approach to kids, drugs, and drug education.* The Lindesmith Center-West.

Rosenberg, S. D. (1979). *Relaxation training and a differential assessment of alcoholism.* Unpublished doctoral dissertation. California School of Professional Psychological, San Diego, CA: University Microfilms No. 8004362.

196 Bibliography

Ross, D. D., Bundy, E., & Kyle, D. W. (1993). *Reflective teaching for student empowerment*. New York: Macmillan.
Salend, S. J., & Whittaker, C. R. (1992). Group evaluation: A collaborative, peer-mediated behavior management system. *Exceptional Children, 59*, 203-209.
Sampson, R. J., & Lauritsen, C. (1997). Racial and ethnic disparities in crime and criminal justice in the United States. In Michael Tonry (Ed.). *Ethnicity, crime, and immigration*. Chicago: University of Chicago Press.
Schinker, S., Botvin, G., & Orland, M. A. (1991). *Substance abuse in children and adolescents: Evaluation and intervention*. Newbury Park, CA: Sage Publications.
Schultz, J. L. (1990). Cooperative learning: The first year. *Educational Leadership, 47* (4), 43-45.
Shade, B. J. (1989). The influence of perceptual development on cognitive style: Cross ethnic comparison. *Early Child Development and Care,* 51, 137-155.
Shade, B. J., & Edward, P. (1987). Ecological correlation of the educative style of African-American children. *Journal of Negro Education, 56* (1), 88-89.
Shedler, J., & Block, J. (1990). Adolescent drug use and psychological health: A longitudinal inquiry. *American Psychologist, 45*, 612-230.
Short, J. F. (1997). Poverty, ethnicity, and violent crime. Boulder, CO: Westview.
Sisson, R. W. (1981). *The effect of three relaxation procedures on tension reduction and subsequent drinking of inpatient alcoholics*. Unpublished doctoral dissertation, Southern Illinois University at Carbondale, Carbondal, IL: University Microfilm No. 8122668.
Skager, R., & Austin, G. (1998). *Sixth Biennial California Student Substance Use Survey*, Sacramento, CA: Office of the Attorney General, State of California.
Slavin, R. E. (1991). *Using student team learning*. Baltimore, MD: Johns Hopkins University, The Center for Social Organization of Schools.

Slavin, R. E., & Oickle, E. (1981). Effects of cooperative learning teams on student achievement and race relations: Treatment by race interactions. *Sociology of Education*, 54, 174-180.

Sloan, T. L. (1992). Influence of male teachers on elementary school children. *Sex Roles*, 26 (4), 120-126.

Smart, R. C. (1974). Employed alcoholics treated voluntarily and under constructive coercion: A follow-up study. *Quarterly Journal of Studies on Alcohol*, 35, 196-209.

Smith, V. E. (1993). Three reasons to keep "hustling." In Ingrassia, *Endangered Family, Newsweek*, 122.

Smith, V. W. (1993). Two dads and a dream - but not illusions. Newsweek, 122, 21. (In Ingrassia, *Endangered Family, Newsweek*, 122, 1993).

Stewart, J., Meier, K., & England, R. (1989). In quest of role models: Change in Black teacher representations in urban school districts, 1968-1986. *Journal of Negro Education*, 58, (2) 140-152.

Stuart, R. B. (1989). Social learning theory: A vanishing or expanding presence? Psychology: A *Journal of Human Behavior*, 26 (1) 35-50.

Taylor, G. R. (1991). Social competence and the early school transition: Risk and protective factors for African-American children. *Education and Urban Society*, 24 (1), 15-26.

Taylor, G. R. (1972). Toward a model K-12 program in drug education. *Association of California School Administrators*, 1 (4), 28-32.

Taylor, G. R. (1992). *Impact of social learning theory on educating deprived/minority children.* Clearinghouse for Teacher Education. (ERIC Document Reproduction Service No. Ed. 349260). Washington, DC.

Taylor, G. R. (1993). *Black male project.* Report submitted to Sinclair Lane Elementary School. Baltimore, MD

Taylor, G. R. (1994). *Three evaluation reports on evaluating social skills of young African-American males.* Reports submitted to Sinclair Lane Elementary School, Baltimore, MD.

Taylor, G. R. (1997). *Curriculum strategies: Social skills intervention for young African-American males.* Westport, CN: Praeger.

Thomas, P. (1995). One in 3 young Black men in the justice system. The *Washington Post*, October 5.

Tobler, N. S., & Stratton, H. H. (1997). Effectiveness of school based drug prevention programs: A meta analysis of the research. *The Journal of Primary Prevention*, 18 (1), 71-128.

Tomlinson, S. (1988). Why Johnny can't read: Critical theory and special education. *European Journal of Special Needs Education*, 3, 45-58.

Tharp, R. G. (1989). Psychocultural variables and constraints: Effects on teaching and learning in schools. *American Psychologists*, 44 (2), 349-359.

The National Association of State Boards of Education. (1992). Alexandria, VA: Author.

Tucker, J., Jalie, A., Donovan, D., & Marlatt, G. A. (1999). *Changing addictive behavior: Bridging clinical and public health strategies.* New York: The Guilford Press.

U. S. Department of Health and Human Services. (1999) *Substance Abuse and Mental Health Administration, Center for Substance Abuse Prevention. Young teens: Who they are and how to communicate with them about alcohol and other drugs.* Rockville, MD: U. S. Department of Health and Human Services.

U. S. Department of Justice, Bureau of Justice Statistics. (1993). *Sentencing in the federal courts: Does race matter? The transition to sentencing guidelines*, 1986-1990.

U. S. General Accounting Office. (1990). *Drug education: School-based programs seen as useful but impact unknown.* Report to the Chairman, Committee on Governmental Affairs, U. S. Senate, Washington, DC: U. S. States General Accounting Office.

U. S. General Accounting Office. (1992). *Adolescent drug use prevention: Common features of promising community programs.* Report to the Chairman, Subcommittee on Select Education, Committee on Labor,House of Representatives. Washington, DC: U. S. General Accounting Office.

U. S. General Accounting Office. (1993). *Drug use among youth: No simple answers to guide prevention.* Washington, DC: U. S. General Accounting Office.

Vasquez, J. A. (1991). *Cognitive style and academic advisement in cultural diversity and the schools: Consensus and controversy.* (Edited by J. Lynch, C. Modgil, and S. Modgil). London: Falconer Press.

Vincent, J. P. (1990). The Biology of Emotions. Cambridge, MA: Basil Blackwell.

Vincent, S. (1993). Drug war claiming "entire generation" of young Blacks. *USA Today*.

Vygotsky, L. S. (Use Moll, IBN). (1991). *The material and the social. Series on cognitive development.* Clearinghouse on Teacher Education (ED. 352186.

Wake County Public School System. (1989). *School/community helping hands project: A plan to combat negative influences on Black male youth.* Raleigh, NC.

Walker, H. M., Irvin, L.K, Noell, J.E, & Singer, G.H. S. (1992). A construct score approach to the assessment of social competence. *Behavior Modification,* 16 (4), 449-452.

Weiner, R. L., Prichard, C., et al. (1993). Evaluation of drug-free schools and community programs. *Evaluation Review,* 17 (5), 488-503.

White, D., & Pitts, M. (1998). Educating young people about drugs: A systematic review. *Addiction,* 93 (10), 1475-1487.

Wiley, R. (1991). *Why Black people tend to shout.* Washington, DC: Carroll Publishing Group.

Witken, H. (1973). *Some implications of research on cognitive style and problems for education.* In personality and learning: Hood and Stoughton.

Wood, J. W. (1984). *Adapting instruction for the mainstream.* Columbus, OH: Charles E. Merrill.

Wright, W. J. (1992). The endangered Black male child. *Educational Leadership,* 49 (4), 14-17.

About The Author

George R. Taylor, Ph.D. is Professor of Special Education and Chairperson Emeritus of the Department of Special Education at Coppin State College, and CORE Faculty, The Union Institute and University. His knowledge and expertise in the areas of Research and Special Education are both locally and nationally renown. He has made significant contributions through Research and Publications in the areas of Special Education, Research, and Education. Additionally, Dr. Taylor has directed several large Federal Research grants and conducted numerous workshops and seminars throughout the country.

Index